How to Train Singers

How to Train Singers

Featuring Illustrated "Natural" Techniques and Exercises

Larra Browning Henderson

Parker Publishing Company, Inc.
West Nyack, New York

© 1979 by

PARKER PUBLISHING COMPANY, INC.

West Nyack, New York

Library of Congress Cataloging in Publication Data

Henderson, Larra Browning
    How to train singers.

    Includes bibliographical references and index.
    1. Singing—Instruction and study.   I. Title.
MT920.H46   784.9'32   78-10950
ISBN 0-13-435511-3

Printed in the United States of America

Dedication

This book is gratefully dedicated to the Giver of all talent and the Creator of the greatest musical instrument—the human voice; and to Maude Douglas Tweedy, the greatest teacher I ever had the privilege of working with, in Europe or the United States. She saved my voice and in doing so saved my life.

Foreword

by Heston L. Wilson, M.D.
Associate Clinical Professor
University of California at San Diego

Medicine provides many hobby opportunities within one's specialty. My interest in otolaryngology, or ear, nose, and throat, began through music. My activity as a former professional—and now avid amateur—woodwind musician fostered an interest in singing.

Through my musical contacts, many instrumentalists as well as singers sought my professional advice. I soon learned that the production of a good singing voice is, in almost all respects, like that of producing outstanding tone on the clarinet or other woodwind or brass instruments. The breath control is the same, the "inside smile" is the same, as are most of the other factors Larra Browning Henderson presents. The major difference is that the woodwind musician uses his reed, or reeds in the case of the oboe family, and the brass player his lips vibrating on a column of air, to produce the tone. The singer and speaker use their vocal cords.

The reed or lips suffer little when misused. The musician may lose his job, but will, hopefully, find a teacher who will set him on the right path. The singer can, on the other hand, damage the vocal cords by misuse. The singer, therefore, must more often seek the otolaryngologist when problems related to singing arise. Fortunately, it is seldom that a singer or speaker must stop his or her career due to laryngeal pathology. Appropriate medical or surgical management, along with proper teaching, can often bring the voice to its normal state. Before working with Larra Browning Henderson I often found myself in two roles. Not only was I treating the medical problem, but also trying with limited time to teach proper vocal habits. Now, by sending the singer or speaker to her or one of her protegées, I can be reassured that the proper voice training will be instituted.

Larra Browning Henderson will mention that the background of this technique is based on the teachings of Dr. Frank E. Miller as they were given to Maude Douglas Tweedy. Dr. Miller's work remains in the darkened archives of medical history, but much credit was given to him for his advanced knowledge of the human voice.

Larra Browning Henderson gives all the credit, and kindly so, to Dr. Miller and Maude Douglas Tweedy. Her technique brings together this scientific foundation and her forty years of experience as a Wagnerian soprano, teacher, and lecturer. It has been my pleasure to have thoroughly tested her technique through patients I have sent to her or one of her protegées.

She stresses that the singing and speaking voice are the same, and I hope that her book will find its way to speakers and teachers of drama and public speaking. The otolaryngologist will find her book extremely useful in diagnosing the problems of the voice he is treating, and, most of all, the teacher of singing will find here an unparalleled text for the teaching of voice.

The voice has become an increasingly important facet in our daily lives. The modes of vocal communication have increased fantastically. Who does not daily use a telephone, tape recorder, or dictaphone? At the same time, television, radio and movies have created a need for knowledge of the voice. Technological advances in medicine have given us many new insights to study the voice.

Dr. Frank E. Miller's book is difficult reading for anyone without a fair degree of medical background. Maude Douglas Tweedy didn't write a book. Larra Browning Henderson writes in a style that holds the interest of the beginning student of voice as well as of the advanced student, the teacher, and the otolaryngologist. This should make this book the standard for all those interested in the voice.

What This Book Can Do For You

This book will show you how to train singers to use their voices with versatility, freedom, ease, endurance, and without discomfort in the throat. Whether belting Broadway show tunes or singing Bach, opera, or folk music, the technique described in the following chapters guarantees longevity for the voice. If you have a student who has a damaged or "sick" voice it will give clues to help in its restoration.

The goal of this book is to aid in building the voice, providing a step-by-step method to achieve this end. There are over fifty illustrations that show what is correct and, in many cases, what is incorrect (position of body, jaw, mask, tongue, head, etc.) for the best possible production of tone. The more than fifty exercises—notated and described as to their *correct* execution—are vital to mastering the singing technique. I have been very specific, for example, in giving the exact exercises to eliminate uneven vibrato, nasality, and many other vocal problems in Chapter 8. Exercises to develop the ability of changing vocal colors in singing texts are spelled out very clearly in Chapter 11.

The key to correct use of the voice is a solid technique. The goal of the technique you will read about here is to enable you to know the abilities and limitations of the voice through experiencing its proper use. Doing this requires an understanding of the workings of the mind and the body, and it is hoped that this book will help to provide this understanding.

You are building responses in the body. You begin with conscious effort and, as these responses become automatic, you add more layers of conscious efforts, which also will become automatic. This is what is meant by a solid technique—one which is automatic.

All of these exercises agree with the natural coordination of the human anatomy. They have been developed to aid the voice student in acquiring proper coordination so that the autonomic nervous system will eventually take over. As you study and use these exercises, you will develop an instinctive sense of timing as to when new and/or more difficult exercises should be used.

As you may realize, many teachers of voice use only scales on vowels to teach vocal technique. The beauty of the technique described in this book is that *consonants* have been scientifically chosen to bring the adjoining vowels into their correct seat.

The technique begins with a core group of exercises which are used by everyone, beginner to advanced. These exercises work on all the various parts of the voice (and, indeed the whole body), and are used daily to warm up the many muscles involved in singing. These are described in detail and are musically notated.

There are, in addition, advanced exercises which will help you meet the demands of different types of literature and help build great stamina. If these exercises are practiced correctly and with knowledge of the principles involved, the singer will advance in the technique at a fairly progressive rate. For those of you who have students with specific vocal problems, there is a chapter devoted to this subject.

This book can be of great value to students of voice, but they must realize that there is no substitute for the trained ear of a teacher. The book can also be used by speech therapists, actors, ministers, lawyers, or by anyone else who uses his voice in his profession—and who doesn't? (We are told by laryngologists that more problems arise with the voice through poor speaking habits than with poor singing.)

All of us must, at some time, appear before an audience—an audience of one for an all-important job interview, or on the stage before thousands. There is no better way to develop poise and self-confidence than through singing.

One of the important points stressed in this book is that a speaker and a singer require exactly the same technique. The only difference between singing and speaking is rhythm and sustaining of tones.

By using the technique in this book, you should become a healthier person. Using the voice is an *athletic activity*. It requires good posture, proper breathing and muscular control. All good teachers of voice encourage vigorous athletics as part of good voice production, since using the voice requires the use of so many muscle groups. In lung disease, for instance, singing provides an excellent means of pleasantly increasing the lung capacity and control. In heart diseases, many scientific studies are coming out showing that a lack of oxygen in the system may be the cause of hardening of the arteries. What better way is there to keep healthy than singing—where deep breathing is absolutely mandatory?

I consider the vocal instrument (which is the entire body) to be divided into three general categories:

1. Breathing and Total Body Support
2. Inside Smile
3. Focus

Correct breathing and support are imperative to insure an even vibrato; what I call the "inside smile" gives warmth to the tone, and focus adds carrying power. Within this book are described over fifty exercises, each of which aids in developing one or more of these categories.

How grateful I have been for having had instructors who knew the *virtue of restraint*. They were so wise in their tutelage. The professional successes that have been mine all came about through concentrated study and guidance of my voice by my teacher, who used the most basic and instructive vocal technique, I believe, available to the student today.

The technique which is described in this book was developed within the framework of the teachings of Dr. Frank E. Miller as they were given to my teacher, Maude Douglas Tweedy, who was then a singer, more than seventy years ago. Dr. Miller was at one time a professional singer himself, in New York City. After becoming a highly respected laryngologist, he addressed himself to the basic problems of the singing and speaking voice and published his findings which scientifically explained why many vocal problems exist and how to correct them.[1] He made detailed studies of the mechanics and physiology of the singing voice and ultimately developed a technique that was compatible with good singing, as well as therapeutic exercises to correct vocal problems. Dr. Miller's background enabled him to establish a reputation among such diverse types of singers as Enrico Caruso and Al Jolson.

This combination of a medical doctor and professional singer laid the foundation for what I believe is the uniqueness and great importance of this technique: it will be physically freeing (and even therapeutic) to the vocal mechanism and will also help to provide a beautiful sound. What more can be asked from a vocal technique?

Dr. Miller and Maude Douglas Tweedy were responsible for the early work, and like any dynamic theory, this basic work has constantly been developed further by others—including myself, my associates, and my students who are now teaching. New "beauties" of the technique insofar as they relate to every problem that arises are constantly being found, but always within the framework originally formulated by Dr. Miller.

Following my own success, both with my own singing career and with teaching, I felt compelled to set the technique down in a book as a guide for those who follow me. There are such vague ideas—and *misinformation*—being given to students concerning the voice that I wanted to share this "foolproof" technique which has served me so well all these years.

In the forty years that I have taught voice, I have heard many voices that have been physically damaged because they were not being used in a way

---

[1] Frank E. Miller, *Vocal Art Science* (New York, G. Schirmer, Inc., 1922), Frank E. Miller, *The Voice* (New York, G. Schirmer, Inc., 1910).

which was compatible with the natural musical instrument. Vocal technique *must be* compatible with natural physiology and anatomy.

I once had an instructor who pinched my hyoid bone and thyroid cartilage apart and also sat on my back while I sang. Tears streamed down my face lesson after lesson. In less than six months I completely lost my voice from G above middle C down, and from high A-flat up. Prior to that time, I had always had a high C and a solid A below middle C. I had been singing lyric spinto roles in *Aida, Tosca*, and *La Forza del Destino* with ease; my voice was tending toward the dramatic soprano literature as well. When I received a scholarship to study in New York, I thought I would be in the best of all possible professional hands; but I soon learned differently.

I continued to study with this instructor, however, for the rest of the school term. I then left the conservatory because of this horrifying experience and searched New York City for three years for the most competent, sensitive and intelligent voice instructor I could find.

The search ended when I entered the studio of Maude Douglas Tweedy, and it was through her technique that I was able to regain my vocal range and make rapid progress. Within six weeks of beginning to work with her (working three and four times a week), I auditioned for the soprano solo position at the largest Jewish temple in New York City, and I was chosen. It was, of course, a steady climb up from there to Europe, Sir Adrian Boult and much more. Throughout my twenty-five year singing career I never left the technique which Maude Douglas Tweedy gave me—*so I know it works!* I judged the teachers with whom I worked in Vienna, Munich, and Zurich on how closely their techniques paralleled this technique.

This book will tell you how to guard the vocal instrument. A singer should *never* experience any discomfort in the laryngeal area. By using this book, the teacher will be able to answer practically every question having to do with the production of tone.

I pray that the results from studying this book will be as helpful and exciting for you as learning the technique has been for me and many others.

Larra Browning Henderson

Acknowledgments

Although it would be impossible to list all the people who have helped to make this book a reality, I am especially indebted:

To my devoted husband, Glen E. Henderson, athletic director and coach, from whom I gained much knowledge which is so applicable to singing;

To our two sons, Dr. Robert G. Henderson, dentist, and Dr. Richard L. Henderson, psychiatrist, whose knowledge in their respective fields has helped me greatly;

To the late Dr. Harry J. Lowen, whose encouragement and interest helped to introduce me to the study of anatomy and physiology of the voice;

To Dr. Myron Talbert, surgeon, whose two daughters studied with me over a period of years and who insisted that I get this technique down in a book because of his own observation of its validity and success;

To Harriet, his wife, who actually began the typing of the book;

To Dr. Heston Wilson, Otolaryngologist, who has been unfailing in his support in getting the writing of this technique down where it would be available to singers, speakers, and laryngologists;

To Beryl Barrowman, who handled all my publicity throughout my career and who was persistent in urging me to get this technique down in print;

To Penny Munroe, my secretary, whose patience and efforts made it possible to get the book finished;

To my excellent photographer, Robert Aiston, and to Ronald Imming, who notated all of the exercises for me;

To Lynne Henderson, who has spent many hours in helping me verbalize the text so it may be understood by the amateur as well as by the professional. In addition, she is responsible for much of the art work in the book;

To all of my students for their help and patience with me in rescheduling lessons, etc., so that I would have time to write this book;

And finally, to John Lasher, who has been a student of mine for more than twenty years. He was of great editorial assistance in the final draft of this book and also prepared the charts and index. For this I will be eternally grateful!

May the contents of this book help all those who sing, for "he who sings, prays twice." (St. Augustine)

LBH

Contents

Foreword   5

What This Book Can Do For You   7

Pronunciation Guide   19

List of Illustrations   21

*Chapter 1 – Practical Tips on the Care and Preservation of
the Singing Voice*   27

How Physical Health Affects the Voice   30
Key Points to Remember   30

*Chapter 2 – First Steps Toward Development of a Healthy
Singing Technique*   33

Prerequisites—A Musical Ear and a Keen Eye   33
Listening and Watching   34
Finding a Voice Teacher   34
The Case Against Combining Opposing Techniques   35
The Inside Smile   35
The Serious Student   40
Learning Devices and Facilities   41
Key Points to Remember   42

Chapter   3 – Anatomy and Physiology: The Foundations of
Correct Technique   **43**

The Teacher's Vocabulary   44
The Nose   44
The Oral Cavity   47
The Pharynx   48
The Larynx   50
The Lungs and Chest   52
The Diaphragm   53
Key Points to Remember   55

Chapter   4 – How to Develop Correct Body Alignment
for Vocal Production   **57**

We Sing with Our Whole Body   57
The Shoulders, Chest and Head   59
The Exercise for Straight Shoulders and
Wide Chest   59
The Swayback Exercise   60
The Head Position   62
Total Body Coordination   63
Key Points to Remember   63

Chapter   5 – Developing Breath Control and Support to
Insure Well-Projected Vocal Production   **65**

Vocal Projection (Volume) is the Result of
Consistent and Concentrated Practice   67
Vocal Line and its Development   67
Three Vocal Ranges   68
Key Points to Remember   70

Chapter   6 – The Seven Basic Exercises for Developing
Vocal Artistry   **71**

Hook Exercise   71
Hee-ah Exercise   74

Kee-kay and Kee-kah Exercises 75
Flah-flah-nee Exercise 76
Ning-ee and Ning-ah Exercises 78
Ng Exercise 79
Preh Exercise 81

Chapter 7 – Advanced Exercises For Developing the Voice to Its Fullest Potential 85

Hook Exercise (Variation) 85
Hawk Exercise 86
Circle-Arm Breath Exercise 86
S-s-s Breath Exercise 89
Back Breath Exercise 90
Ballet Stretch 91
Kah-kay-kee-koh-koo Exercise 91
Kee-kah-kee Exercise 92
Koo Exercises 93
Flah-flah-ning-ah Exercise 95
Rag Doll Exercise 95
Wide-Snuff Exercise 96
Hee-ah and Hah-ah Exercises 97
Waw-ee 98
Ng-ee-ay-ah 99
Snuff zoh zah Exercises 100
Sh-sh-sh and Ng-ng-ng Exercises 102
Nee-oh Exercise 103
Nee-oh-(ay)-(ah)-(eye) Exercise 104
Five-Part Exercise 104
Part 1: Ning-ee and Ning-ah 105
Part 2: Heady Nee and Nee-ah 105
Parts 3 and 4: Thee-thah and Thah-thee 106
Part 5: Nee-ah-ee-ah-ee-ah-ee Exercise 108
Ming mee Exercises 110
Lah bay dah may nee poh too 111
Mee-oh Exercise 111
Mee-ah Exercise (1) 112
Nee-ah Exercise (2) 112
Nee-ah Exercise (3) 113

**Chapter 8 – Exercises and Techniques for Correcting
Vocal Problems**   **115**

Nasality   116
Ah-ah-ah Exercise   119
Rolled Tongue Exercise   119
The Irregular Vibrato   121
Exercises to Correct the Irregular Vibrato   122
Hum-mee and Hum-mah Exercise   122
Waw-ee-ah Exercise   123
Hum-Portamento Exercises   123
Tongue Problems   123
Exercises Used to Correct Tongue Irregularities   124
Ng-ah Exercise   127
Gah Exercise   127
Incorrect Lip Formation   128
Vocal Problems Originating with the Jaw   130
The Shaking Jaw   132
Sit-Up Exercise   133
The Stiff Jaw   133
Fah-ee-ah-ee and Fee-ah-ee-ah Exercises   134
Hum-mah and Hum-may Exercises   134
Kah-kee-koh Exercise   135
The Jutting Jaw   136
Vocal Nodes   136
Hah-hay-hee-hoh-hoo Exercise   137
Flah-flah Exercise   138
Mah-mah Exercise   139
Hum-ee and Hum-ah Exercises   140
Vocal Problems in General   140

**Chapter 9 – Singing Vowels and Consonants: A Comprehensive
Technique for Correct Diction**   **143**

Every Vowel Has its Own Shape   143
Various Vowel Problems   144
Consonants Lead out the Vowel   146
Consonants with Duration-Voiced   149
Consonants with Duration-Unvoiced   150
Consonants with Less Duration-Voiced   150
Consonants with Less Duration-Unvoiced   150
Key Points to Remember   150

Chapter 10 – Learning to Sing the Vocal Text **153**

The Role of Vocal and Dramatic Coaches 154
Technique First and Then Expression 155
Key Points to Remember 156

Chapter 11 – Tested and Effective Performance Technique **157**

Stage Fright 159
Without a Good Technique There Is No
   Interpretation 159
How Do We Get These Colors? 160
The Warm and/or Loving Tone Color 161
The Pants Role 162
Lullaby From *Songs and Dances of Death* by
   Mussorgsky 163
Schumann's *Frauenliebe Und Leben* 163
Character Roles 164
The Belting or "Broadway" Tone 165
Key Points to Remember 167

Chapter 12 – Techniques and Exercises that Produce Dynamic and Exciting Choral Performances **169**

Warm-Ups are Imperative 169
General Choral Comments 175
Contests and Festivals 177
Musical Theater 177
A Special Note to Choir Directors 178
Singing on Mikes 179
The Importance of Church Organists 180
Key Points to Remember 180

Chapter 13 – How to Deal with Problems of the Throat: Case Studies and Exercises **183**

Each Vocal Problem is Unique 184
General Causes of Vocal Problems 184
Two Case Histories 186

Basic Steps   194
Dealing with Surgery   194
What to Do After a Tonsillectomy   195
Key Points to Remember   196

Chapter 14 – Key Questions on This Technique—
With Answers   **197**

Conclusion   **211**

Appendix 1   Marchesi in Detail: The Use of Supplementary
Exercises   **215**

Appendix 2   Definitions   **221**

Appendix 3   Exercise Chart   **223**

Breathing and Body Coordination   223
Strengthening the Soft Palate   223
Coordination of Tongue and Jaw   224
Focus   224
Bridge Over Ranges   224
Extension of Range   224
Remove Shrillness   224
Developing Staccato   225
Relating Vocalises to Sung Texts   225
Tongue   225

Index   **227**

Pronunciation Guide

Because many readers of this book possibly have not been exposed to the International Phonetic Alphabet, all exercises and examples given in this book use the following as a vowel pronunciation guide:

a	as in	at
ah	as in	father
aw	as in	awful
ay	as in	hate
ee	as in	easy
eh	as in	every
eye	as in	eye
ih	as in	it
oh	as in	know
oo	as in	moon
uh	as in	up

Note Regarding Exercises

All exercises in the book are notated in the key of C major (except for waw-ee) for uniformity. It is possible, however, that some, as explained in the book, will start in various keys other than C. It is imperative that each exercise be tailored to start in the lower middle range of the particular voice for which it is being used.

List of Illustrations

Figure   **Page**

Chapter 2

1	Photo – Dropped Jaw and Mask (incorrect)	36
2a	Photo – Fluted lips (incorrect)	36
2b	Photo – Rounded lips (''oh'') (correct)	36
3a	Photo – Position of mask while using inside smile (female)	37
3b	Photo – Position of mask while using inside smile (male)	38
4	Photo – Grimace (incorrect)	39
5	Photo – Deadpan expression (incorrect)	39

Chapter 3

6a	Medical Drawing – The Tongue and its relationship to the Vocal Tract	45
6b	Medical Drawing – Muscles of the Tongue	46
6c	Medical Drawing – Muscles Connecting the Tongue to other Structures	46
7	Medical Drawing – Pharynx: Nasopharynx, Oropharynx, Hypopharynx	49
8	Medical Drawing – Larynx	51
9	Medical Drawing – Vocal folds (inhalation)	51
10	Medical Drawing – Diaphragm	53
11a	Medical Drawing – Diaphragm (Inhalation)	54
11b	Medical Drawing – Diaphragm (Exhalation)	54

Chapter 4

12	Photo – Correct body alignment (knees flexed)	58
13	Photo – Incorrect body alignment (stiff knees)	58
14	Photo – Correct position of head and shoulders	59

Figure   **Page**

15   Photo – Rounded shoulders, sunken chest, head and neck
              pulled forward (incorrect)   59
16   Photo – Exercise position pulling shoulders back   60
17   Photo – Swayback (incorrect)   61
18   Photo – Exercise to eliminate swayback   61
19   Photo – Chin pulled up (incorrect)   62
20   Photo – Chin pressed down (incorrect)   62

Chapter 5

21   Music – Double prime octave   68

Chapter 6

22   Medical Drawing – Abdominal muscles (side view)   72
23   Music – He-ah   74
24   Music – Kee-kay and Kee-kah   75
25   Music – Flah-flah-nee   77
26   Photo – Tip of tongue pulled up on ''l'' and ''n'' (incorrect) 78
27   Photo – Nee, lower lip pulled in (incorrect)   78
28   Music – Ning-ee and ning-ah   79
29   Music – Ng 54321   79
30   Music – Ng 5432123454321   79
31   Music – Ng (descending octave)   79
32   Photo – Correct position of mouth and tongue while singing
              ''ng'' exercise   81
33   Music – Preh   82
34   Photo – Correct position of lips while singing ''preh'' exercise 82
35   Photo – Nose wrinkled while singing ''preh'' exercise (incor-
              rect)   82

Chapter 7

36a   Music – Hawk   86
36b   Music – Hawk   86
37   Photo – Preparation for circle-arm breath (back view)   88
38   Photo – Arm crossing in front of body during inhalation of
              circle-arm breath   88
39   Photo – Position between inhalation and exhalation during
              circle-arm breath   88

Figure		**Page**
40	Photo – Arm coming down during exhalation of circle-arm breath	88
41	Music – Kah-kay-kee-koh-koo	91
42	Music – Kee-Kah-Kee	93
43	Music – Koo	93
44	Music – Koo-koo-koo-koo-koo	94
45	Photo – Rounded lips while singing ''oo''	94
46	Music – Flah-flah-ning-ah	95
47	Photo – Face position for wide snuff	97
48	Music – Hee-ah and hah-ah (heady)	98
49	Music – Waw-ee	98
50	Music – Ng-ee-ay-ah	99
51	Music – Snuff-zoh, snuff-zah, snuff hum	100
52	Music – Snuff zoh, zah	100
53	Music – Zoh, zah	100
54	Music – Zay-luh, zah luh	100
55	Music – Zay-luh, zah luh	100
56	Music – Shh-shh-shh	102
57	Music – Ng-ng-ng	102
58	Music – Nee-oh-ee-oh	103
59	Music – Nee-oh-ay, nee-oh-ah, nee-oh-eye	104
60	Music – Ning-ee, ning-ah	105
61	Photo – Rolled upper lip position for part one of five-part exercise	105
62	Music – Nee and nee-ah	106
63	Music – Thee thah	106
64	Music – Thah thee	107
65	Photo – Tongue position for parts three and four of five-part exercise	107
66a	Music – Nee-ah-ee-ah-ee-ah-ee	108
66b (1)	Music – Nee and nah	109
66b (2)	Music – Nee-ah-ee-ah-ee	109
67a	Music – Ming ming ming	110
67b	Music – Mee mee mee	110
68	Music – Lah-bay-dah-may-nee-poh-too	111
69	Music – Mee-oh	111
70	Music – Nee-ah (#1)	112
71	Music – Nee-ah (#2)	113
72	Music – Nee-ah (#3)	113

Figure **Page**

Chapter 8

73	Medical Drawing – Soft palate (relaxed)	117
74	Medical Drawing – Soft palate (active)	118
75	Music – Nee and nah	120
76	Photo – Tongue and mask positions for rolled tongue exercise	121
77	Music – Hum-mee and hum-mah	122
78a	Music – Hum-portamento	123
78b	Music – Hum-portamento	123
79	Photo – Correct position of tip of tongue	124
80	Photo – Pulled up tongue (incorrect)	125
81	Photo – Pressed tongue (incorrect)	125
82	Photo – Grooved tongue (incorrect)	126
83	Photo – Pulled back tongue (incorrect)	126
84a	Photo – Facial position while using inside smile (male)	128
84b	Photo – Facial position while using inside smile (female)	129
84c	Photo – Facial position while using inside smile (female)	129
85	Photo – Short upper lip	130
86a	Photo – Correct swing of the jaw	131
86b	Photo – Jaw jutting forward (incorrect)	131
87	Photo – Jaw moving to the side (incorrect)	132
88	Music – Hee-ah (sit-up)	133
89	Music – Fah-ee-ah-ee, fee-ah-ee-ah	134
90	Music – Hum-mah, hum-may	135
91	Music – Kah-kee-koh	135
92	Medical Drawing – Vocal folds with nodes	137
93	Music – Hah-hay-hee-hoh-hoo	137
94	Music – Flah-flah-flah	138
95	Music – Kee-kay-kee-kah	139
96	Music – Mah mah mah	139
97	Music – Hum-ee- hum-ah	140

Chapter 9

98	Medical Drawing – Muscles used while singing the "preh" exercise	145

Figure *Page*

Chapter 12

99	Photo – Body alignment—knees locked (incorrect)	172
100	Photo – Correct body alignment	172
101	Photo – Correct sitting position for choral rehearsal	176
102	Music – Comfortable Ranges and Maximum Ranges for the Average Choir Member	176

1

PRACTICAL TIPS ON THE CARE

AND PRESERVATION

OF THE SINGING VOICE

The foremost foundation for building a fine and beautiful voice is a healthy and physiologically sound vocal mechanism with which to work. The young voice can be considered a sort of "tabula rasa," a beautiful base upon which a smooth, vibrant sound can be developed; but only if done so with restraint, and with a clear understanding of a physiologically sound technique, such as the one described in this book.

Therefore, the first step toward a solid technique is the care and preservation of the voice. A person knows that all the parts of his car must be functioning correctly before it will perform to its maximum ability. If the wheels are out of alignment, or any part of the engine needs repairs which are not made, severe damage may be done. So it is with the voice. Improper care and maintenance of the voice will result in permanent damage. However, unlike a car, the parts of which can be replaced, man is given only one set of vocal cords. Do not *abuse* them—learn how to *use* them. That is what this book is about.

This lesson of abuse was brought home to me very early in my singing career when I was a sophomore in college. A group of us were singing "just for fun" out in the cold night air. Two of us, high sopranos, were "faking tenor" above all the group. Thank goodness I knew when to stop. The other girl kept singing and singing and singing. When she reached home she was hoarse. For four days she could hardly speak. She went to the laryngologist and he told her she had abused her throat so badly that the vocal cords would probably never be normal again. They never were! She not only lost her singing voice completely, but her speaking voice had a husky quality from then on.

I cannot stress enough the danger of over-singing in the cold night air, cheerleading, and screaming.

A high school junior auditioned for me to hold a place for her in my schedule for the coming year. She had a beautiful high clear singing voice with a lovely high C and a wide range. When I returned in the fall to begin my teaching, she called me to say that she "had lost her voice" during the summer at music camp. I was shocked. She told me that she could only sing to the a' and no higher. I asked her what she had been doing. She explained that they had been rehearsing four to six hours per day, sometimes out in the cold night air.

Music camps should be very aware that the vocal instrument is not like any man-made instrument. I have found in my years of experience of working with high school level singers, that too much has been demanded of them during the summer camp experience. I do not want to leave the impression that I am against summer music camps. They can provide fine musical experiences when the voices with which they are dealing are given first consideration.

During a vocal workshop that I was conducting in the Northeast, a seventeen year old student came to me with a very audible vocal abnormality. His first lesson made it obvious that there were tones that were not normal in his singing. By the second lesson it became evident that there were basic physical problems in the vocal mechanism itself.

I sent him to a laryngologist who relayed the sad message to me that this young student had "bowed" vocal cords. (This is a term referring to a physical deformation that structurally changes the normal shape of the cords. If you were able to see the cords inside the throat, they would look bowed or arch-shaped.) Such a vocal problem, of course, made it almost impossible to even consider a future in voice, since the sounds emanating from his throat were not consistent in pitch, texture, resonance and vibration.

I learned that his problem was not a congenital defect, but one acquired through misuse of his voice by his vocal instructors in his early education. While singing in an all-state chorus, he had almost lost his voice. The vocal literature chosen for this chorus was in too high a range for this young tenor voice. The rehearsal periods were four and five hours a day—*much* too long for young voices. I think we can now understand why his vocal cords were bowed.

When the reed of a clarinet is worn out or damaged, it can be discarded and a new one purchased. *It is not so with the vocal cords*! When the wind instrument player is required to use his lips for an over-extended period of time, he refuses to do so because the muscles involved are unable to be used without limit. When an instrumentalist refuses to play because his lips and tongue are tired, it is accepted, but when a vocalist tries to protect his voice by not singing longer or higher than he should be singing, he is called a ''prima donna'' and literally forced to continue. The singer should be allowed to ''mark'' (i.e., sing a well-supported light tone or sing lightly an octave below the score) the music in rehearsal.

The members of one high school singing group, which was in a large contest, were so over-rehearsed and their throats were hurting them so before the final competition, that the director, with a prescription in her hand, obtained a spray to deaden the pain which was in her singers' throats.

No throat lozenges or any spray which has pain-killing properties should *ever* be used to enable you to continue singing! By using these artificial means, all you are doing is covering up the pain. Through the pain, your body is trying to tell you something—*rest your voice*!

Laryngologists tell us that smoke is very irritating to the vocal cords; it can cause tiny blisters to form. Anyone who is seriously considering a vocal career should not smoke. It not only irritates the cords, but it irritates all of the tissues of the lungs, throat, and nasal cavity. It cuts down the breath capacity and will destroy the top range of the voice.

Laryngologists explain the effect of alcohol on the cords by comparing it to the effect on an alcoholic who sometimes has tiny broken blood vessels under the skin that give him a ruddy complexion. Alcohol affects the cords in the same way. Since alcohol is also a relaxant, when one has a cocktail and demands that the cords keep functioning for speaking or singing, one is adding to the injury.

A singer should never try to speak over the noise in crowded rooms, at parties or in restaurants. Doing so is very hard on the cords. Drinking cold drinks just before singing is detrimental. Even though the liquid does not go over the cords, it tightens the soft palate and the pharyngeal area, both of which are so important.

Cold, air-conditioned air can be disastrous to a singer. When the air passes over the vocal cords, it tightens them. A parallel to this would be a runner who would throw ice water on his legs before a race. Often a pianist will wear warm gloves before performing, and a dancer wears leg warmers all the way to the hips so that the muscles will remain supple and never tight. A singer must be aware that outside conditions have a definite effect on the voice. When he is performing in concert (perhaps with an orchestra) and is sitting on stage waiting to perform, he should be very careful not to allow the body to become chilled. Also, going from a hot stage to a cold dressing room can have disastrous effects on the vocal instrument. *The singer must be aware of all of this and must take precautions to guard against harming the vocal instrument.*

HOW PHYSICAL HEALTH AFFECTS THE VOICE

It is imperative for a singer to do some physical exercise which will strengthen the thoracic cavity and the lower abdominal area. Running or brisk walking are both very beneficial. Swimming is also beneficial as long as you don't keep your head under water and get chlorine into the frontal sinus. Some form of ballet is highly recommended.

It is very important to singers that the hormones be kept in balance through the entire career.

The "Pill": The "pill" definitely affects the voice, some voices more than others.

Thyroid: Thyroid level is also something that a singer should be aware of; it must not be too high or too low. The balance severely affects the voice. When a singer develops a "veil" over the voice, and the upper range is not as facile as it has been, and there is vocal fatigue, it is wise to consult a doctor for the possibility of thyroid dysfunction.

Menstruation: The menstrual cycle can produce changes in the voice. One should not make demands on the voice at critical times. The vocal cords swell during the few days prior to menstruation and during the first days of menstruation. In Europe these are called "respect days" and one is not required to perform. In the United States, where these "respect days" often are not observed, vocal impairments have occurred many times.

Pregnancy: If all is going well during the pregnancy, one is free to sing. After the birth it is important not to begin singing immediately while the body is weakened and fatigued.

Menopause: At the time of menopause a woman's voice may lose its lustre because of a possible hormonal imbalance. It would then be wise to be checked by a gynecologist.

From my personal observations, the longevity of a vocal career is directly related to the care and preservation of the voice.

KEY POINTS TO REMEMBER

1. Since one cannot replace the vocal cords, one must be careful never to abuse them, but instead learn how to use them correctly.
2. In rehearsal, singers should "mark" as often as necessary.

3. One who depends on his voice should stay away from pain-deadening lozenges or sprays, smoking, and alcohol. He must be very careful of noisy rooms and cold areas.

4. Exercise is vital, and one should be aware of the potential effect on the voice of the "pill," thyroid dysfunctions, menstruation, menopause and pregnancy.

2

FIRST STEPS TOWARD DEVELOPMENT
OF A HEALTHY SINGING TECHNIQUE

The instruction and learning processes basic to vocal technique must have their beginnings at a level of complete devotion to the study of singing. The 3-D's of great singing are: Discipline, Direction, and Devotion.

The student of voice should realize the importance of his training and, therefore, the importance of preparing required material and preserving all that he has learned at each lesson by taking down copious and careful notes. Energetic and earnest practice with great attention given to the fine points of the study of voice is the best way of insuring the finest results.

The student should come to his lesson vocally prepared and with a word for word translation of the text into his native tongue. The written text should be practiced independently of the music and then put together with the musical score. This method will allow the student to concentrate on applying the actual technique of singing—preferably the principles discussed in this book. Learning to sing with any technique requires the understanding that it is a detailed and extensive study. A fine vocal technique allows a singer to go on to become a great interpreter of the vocal literature.

There are many vistas in singing open to the student of voice but the fundamentals of technique must be mastered *before* the vocal message can be completely conveyed.

PREREQUISITES—A MUSICAL EAR AND A KEEN EYE

Both the student and the teacher should have an acutely musical ear and a keenly observant eye, which will hear and see the physical coordination which produces a correct sound. What is considered correct or incorrect technique is based on physical sensations. Practicing exercises in front of a mirror allows the student to "see" what he feels so that he can coordinate the two. As the correct coordination becomes a habit, the involuntary nervous system will then be able to take over the singing process and a good performance will come through the use of these sensations.

LISTENING AND WATCHING

During the lesson, the teacher should not be too involved with playing the piano score for the student. Accompanying the student during the lesson is the least important consideration that the instructor should give in teaching vocal technique. *Listening* to the student and *watching* with intensity should be the first considerations given during the lesson. It is wrong for the teacher to be constantly illustrating tones to be sung, because the student may then try to imitate the sound of his teacher's voice. Since each voice is unique, no student should try to imitate any other singer's voice. It is fine to listen to other singers, but one should not try to imitate their sound.

No teacher should sing with the student while he is singing. If he does this, the teacher cannot accurately hear the sound of his student's voice. The correction of faulty technique and faulty muscular coordination, along with confirmation of correct technique and correct muscular coordination, remain the most important accomplishments of the instruction period. The student pays the instructor to *listen* and to *watch,* and to make corrections and suggestions; otherwise, bad technique is allowed to go unchecked.

Some teachers are excellent pianists. Even with this ability, quite often their minds are divided between the accompaniment and the student (which should *not* be). The teacher who plays may also lead the student dynamically and rhythmically, thus creating a dependence upon the teacher, which is difficult to break. This should be carefully watched in order to be avoided.

FINDING A VOICE TEACHER

Before the student can establish a good basic foundation for building his voice, a voice teacher must be found—a voice teacher with the knowledge of a sound and ethical technique.

There is no real basis for the theory that a student should choose his teacher on the premise that a male student should study with a male teacher, and a female study with a female, simply because there are physical differences in the vocal mechanism of each sex. Such a premise is ill-founded. It is true that the laryngeal area of the male usually is larger than that of the female, but the muscles and nerves involved in singing are structurally and dynamically the same. The only differences may lie in chemical effects interacting with the vocal mechanism involving hormones and periodic changes in their levels. Consideration of an instructor based on sex differences is totally unwarranted.

An essential factor in the choosing of a voice teacher is trust. The student should have complete trust in the teacher and be willing to comply with the teacher's instruction. This will guarantee that the learning process will be one of continuous growth. When the student understands the technique he is using and its effects upon the vocal instrument, he should then be able to feel definite progress towards the development of a voice freed to sing with warmth, color, and vibrancy. It is the instructor's calling to free the voice, not to force its growth.

THE CASE AGAINST COMBINING OPPOSING TECHNIQUES

There are many faulty techniques that instructors use, unsuccessfully, to try to build the vocal line. These techniques are not in agreement in their approach with the technique described in this text, and it is best not to try to mix one with the other.

It has been observed that all fine teaching shares the same goals but the methods of obtaining them vary widely. Any combination of different techniques is somewhat like having two architects, each with a different style of designing and engineering, work on the same structure. It is imperative to have just one architect, and likewise, to have one vocal instructor using one technique.

Two examples of techniques which contradict the basic principles of the technique which you will learn from this book are those based on a dropped jaw and mask (Figure 1) and on a fluted lip (Figure 2a). (Even when singing the "oh" (Figure 2b), the lips are never tight.) The "dropped jaw" principle is based on dropping the jaw what I would consider to be too far on any vowel in any range; the "dropped mask" principle allows the mask to drop (with no involvement of the cushions under the eyes or the upper lip) on *all* vowels and all consonants. The jaw which drops too far does not allow for a clean enunciation of text or for the correct sitting of tones; it causes tones to be sung all in one color and many times flat in pitch (especially on the brighter vowel sounds). The bright vowel sounds need a very big back space and an arched soft palate, initiated by the inside smile (Figures 3a and 3b).

THE INSIDE SMILE

In this book I will be using the term "inside smile" consistently. The following is what I mean by this term:

> Close the mouth, but not the teeth (feeling an openness in the whole oral cavity) and smile as though you were smiling at someone across the room, *a smile you do not wish to be noticed by others*. You feel a slight lifting of the cushions under the eyes and a space opening up over the soft palate— you almost feel as though you are going to break into a yawn. The soft

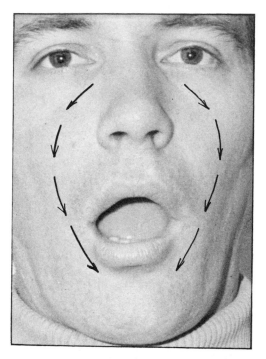

Figure 1
Dropped jaw and mask (incorrect)

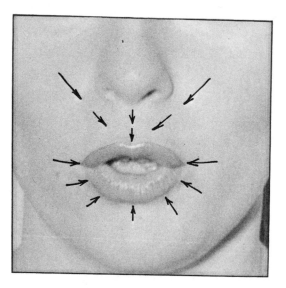

Figure 2a
Fluted lips (incorrect)

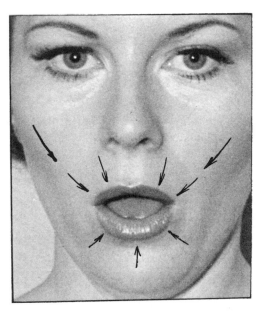

Figure 2b
Rounded lips ("oh") (correct)

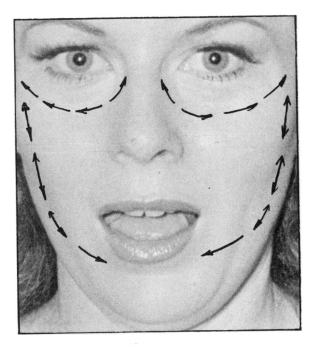

Figure 3a
Position of mask while using inside smile (female)

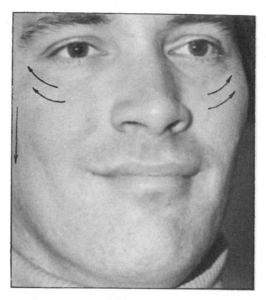

Figure 3b
Position of mask while using inside smile (male)

palate goes up. *You have not pulled it up.* Both are extremely important—the cushions under the eyes and the soft palate.

Lest you try this in the extreme, let me emphasize that the impulse which causes the mask to lift comes from the soft palate (inside smile). The singer smiles a *natural* smile. A grimace (Figure 4), or tightening of the cheek muscles and pulling the corners of the mouth wide, is incorrect. It will cause the tone to be white and tight. The extreme opposite of this is the "dead pan" (Figure 5) where the mask is dropped and one has a very glum look. When you use the inside smile, there is a feeling of "dome" in the oral cavity; there is also a "yawning up" sensation (never a "yawning down" position, i.e., pressure on the back of the throat and the larynx). The same sensation comes into the soft palate area when one is expressing surprise with a slight gasp and the cushions under the eyes lift. When I speak of the inside smile, I am speaking of all of the above.

The inside smile frees the soft palate and other muscles of the oropharynx (See Chapter 3) to act in their most efficient fashion. It also brings the tongue into position for good articulation.

When the jaw is allowed to swing too far on vowel sounds (in all ranges), the "dome" is automatically pulled down and the back spaces are decreased. The "relaxed mask" also affects those spaces and, if used on every vowel, especially the open vowels, those vowels all tend to be sung with the resulting sound of "aw." (This is easy to understand since it is even more difficult to speak "ay" and "ee" with a relaxed mask, the lips rounded and slightly

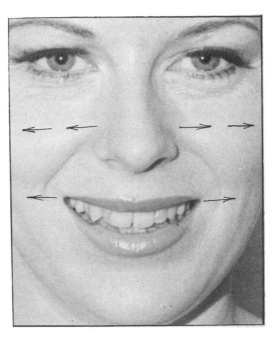

Figure 4
Grimace (incorrect)

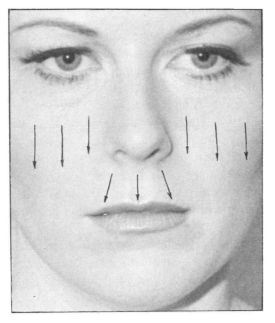

Figure 5
Deadpan expression (incorrect)

closed.) The bright vowels and the aspirant consonants all must employ the "raised mask" (Figure 3)—the "raised mask" being a result of the inside smile. The cushions should be lifted and the upper lip involved from the inside in order to get the correct sound.

The "fluted lip" technique is even more radical in its approach since it requires that the lips remain pursed (without any use of the raised cushions or inside smile) on every tone. Every tone produced by the singer who uses this technique, be it an "ee," "ah," "eh," or "ay," results in a muffled sound. It is impossible to comprehend how such a singer can believe that his audience can understand the language in which he is singing.

THE SERIOUS STUDENT

Along with acquiring good basic technique comes the need to combine the singing of the literature with an accompaniment which flows under, through, and around the vocal score, enhancing it and ultimately allowing the text to sound the way the composer and librettist intended. Since the accompaniment will usually be from a piano, when the student is far enough advanced in his technique, an accompanist should be obtained. (All pianists are not necessarily good accompanists. Often, those who are the best soloists do not have the empathy required for the real rapport necessary between singer and accompanist.)

Building rapport with an accompanist is an involved process and one which cannot be taken lightly. The accompanist can enhance or detract from a singer. The student should rehearse with the accompanist for at least one hour (or more, if possible) between lessons. It is wise to have the accompanist present for the last period of the lesson (after the student is "warmed up") so that the teacher can sit back and view the singer at work with prepared literature. From such a vantage point, the teacher can hear and see everything involved in the student's technique and its interplay with the text and accompaniment; correction of vocal problems can then be made. After the student has become advanced enough to give a recital, he should come "warmed up" to each lesson until the recital is over and sing the complete lesson with the accompanist.

For the serious student anticipating a career in singing, two or three lessons a week should be augmented with at least one coaching lesson. Coaching teaches the real art of phrasing, correct diction in all languages in which the vocal literature is written, as well as interpretation and style.

The teacher of voice and the vocal coach should reinforce each other's work. The teacher should be the "technician," aiding in obtaining the vocal colors, dynamics, and style that the vocal coach is asking for. A coach has generally not been a singer; therefore he should *not* tamper with the singer's technique. After a singer is well established in his technique, he can do with fewer "vocal lessons" and rely more on the ear of a good vocal coach. Along with the coach, the teacher and the student can plan together toward projected ends with confidence that those ends shall eventually be reached.

A student should never overindulge in practicing or rehearsing; in addition, he should choose literature which is most complementary to his present vocal range and capabilities. There is much that he can learn silently through memorizing literature, translating the text if it is in a foreign language, developing the character or envisioning the mood that must be vocally projected to the listener, or simply working through the technique silently. It takes time to understand the text and couple its meaning with the music itself. This is the culmination of all musical ability—a beautiful sound, which, when phrased well, paints a vocal picture that the listener can actually visualize. All of these separate studies which are part of singing take up much time. If the student works on all of the above every day, he will be studying one or two hours a day without even having sung a note.

LEARNING DEVICES AND FACILITIES

In order for a student to study voice effectively, the practice room and the studio should be equipped with certain "tools of the trade."

The practice room should be as soundproof as possible so that the singing will not disturb others in the vicinity and so that others will not disturb the singer. Good acoustics are essential to a good practice room—"good acoustics" meaning that the ceiling should be high (under perfect conditions), and the floor partially carpeted or covered with some sort of material to control erratic bouncing of sounds from surface to surface. The practice facility should also have an in-tune piano available so that the exercises can be practiced while maintaining correct pitch. Of course, the piano is a first requirement when the average student attempts to learn new material. It is quite impossible to learn vocal literature from the bare beginnings without the aid of a piano unless one is endowed with perfect pitch or is an excellent sight reader.

The teacher's studio, like the practice facility, should be soundproof, should have good acoustics, and should be located in a relatively quiet area. Full-length mirrors should be used to allow the student a full view of his entire body from head to toe so that correct body alignment can be maintained.

Hand mirrors should also be part of the studio's equipment, providing the student with a view of the entire face, tongue, teeth, and hard and soft palates. As referred to earlier, he will then be able to establish why the sensation of the tone, incorrect or correct, is where it is. When established, the sensations of correct vocal technique will attain the warmest, most beautiful and controlled tones possible. It is a good idea for the student to have hand mirrors available when practicing. In that way, the feeling of correct vocal technique can remain throughout the practice period just as it should during the lesson.

Another piece of equipment, which some might consider optional but which I feel is helpful, is a tape recorder which can be very useful to the student and the instructor. The student should not be too critical of the sound of his voice coming from the recording device; it is not a true mirror of the sound as a professional recording produced in an acoustically perfect studio would be. If he desires, each lesson can be taped and saved for review. Taping equipment (especially the smaller cassette recorders, which are portable) saves agonizing memory work when the student tries to review all that has happened during each lesson. The teacher may find it to his advantage to have larger reel-to-reel taping devices available in the studio in order to tape studio recitals and/or pieces of vocal literature sung by students which the teacher would like to keep available for future reference. Also, many students have larger tape recorders and would prefer to tape their lessons on a larger machine if one is available in the studio.

KEY POINTS TO REMEMBER

1. A serious student must have: Discipline, Direction, and Devotion.

2. Students and teachers must constantly make use of their ears *and* eyes to be able to coordinate the best sound.

3. A good teacher will give as much attention as possible to what the student is doing, accompanying as little as possible and making sparing use of his own voice during the lesson.

4. A student should not worry as to whether a potential teacher is the same sex as he is, but should have complete trust in whatever teacher he chooses. He should study his teacher's technique *completely* and not try to combine opposing techniques.

3

ANATOMY AND PHYSIOLOGY: THE FOUNDATIONS OF CORRECT TECHNIQUE

Since this technique was developed by a laryngologist through scientific research with his patients, a study of anatomy and physiology is necessary to the understanding of the technique. It is important that anatomy and physiology books be available in the studio and that students take advantage of them so that they may learn just exactly how all of the basic structures work together in singing. Too much emphasis on anatomy and physiology can be harmful in assimilating the vocal technique; but it is important to know the basic anatomy and how it works.

I have always been grateful for my acquaintance with Dr. Harry J. Lowen in New York City during the early part of my career as a singer and teacher. He was responsible for my developing a deeper interest in the functions of the diaphragm and the whole abdominal area while singing. He allowed me to bring in a professional singer, who was working with me at that time, and by means of the fluoroscope I was able to watch these functions. When the student let go of the support of the lower abdominal area, the diaphragm moved up about an inch and a half in its position. This clearly indicated to me the importance of the use of the *complete* abdominal area in supporting the voice. When the student sang a staccato passage, the movement of the diaphragm resembled the ripples which result from throwing a pebble into a placid lake.

It is necessary to discuss the anatomy and physiology of the pharyngeal and facial areas so that the sound of the most perfect and resonant tone can be fully understood. The actions of the tongue, jaw, soft palate, etc., affect the resonance and focus of the spoken and sung tone. After a discussion of anatomy and physiology, the student will have a better understanding of the purpose of each exercise and his goal in practicing it. By constantly repeating these exercises, the student is training the musculature to respond correctly and to allow the tone to "sit" in a position where it is resonant and has complete freedom from tightness in the laryngeal area or in the muscles of the neck.

THE TEACHER'S VOCABULARY

I have always preferred speaking of a tone "sitting" rather than speaking of "placing" the tone. Singing is a constant discovery of new sensations in the head, oral cavity, and chest area in the different ranges of the voice. One has to admit that the voice teacher's vocabulary is peculiar to his profession. When one says "the tone sits front," one feels that sensation forward in the oral cavity and/or nasal cavity. When the tone "sits too far back" the sensation is an entirely different one within the oral cavity and/or nasal cavity. That sensation is no longer in the nasopharynx but in the back part of the oral cavity and is sometimes felt in the throat. *No feeling should ever be in the throat.*

The muscles related to the superstructure of the nose are extremely important to the tone quality and for maintaining strength while singing. When singing correctly, the muscles over the bridge of the nose, across the face, under the eyes, and around the mask (Figure 3) are very much involved; when activated, they allow for good articulation by aiding the arching movement of the soft palate in the "inside smile."

The strength of the facial muscles and of those across the bridge of the nose activates what I term the "inside pull-ups." The innervation of the facial muscles and the action of lifting the cushions under the eyes, the corners of the mouth turned upward, *never outward,* is termed "employing the mask."

The mask—the facial area where the tone sits and where the feeling of tone originates—is especially important when producing bright vowels and aspirant consonants. The cushions are not employed when singing dark vowels, i.e., "oh," "oo," "aw," (Figures 2 a and b), but it is important to note that regardless of whether a vowel is dark or bright, the vowel feels as though it has a connection to the septum (the cartilage separating the two halves of the nose), and there is muscular strength close to the nose. This muscular strength originates from the soft palate and "inside smile," providing the oral cavity with increased room in which tones may resonate and words may be articulated. Such a feeling of space inside the mouth is often referred to as the "arch" or "dome" shape.

THE NOSE

The nose warms and moistens the air. The external nose is very important to the singing voice. Delicate facial muscles can partially open and close the two external nasal passages. When singing properly, the muscles below the eyes rise slightly, as do the muscles of the external nose. These muscles of the external nose rise so slightly that their action is *completely invisible* to a viewer, but the singer definitely feels a resulting strength in the tone. The result is widening of the alae, or side walls of the nasal openings. This opens the nasal passageway and in turn improves the resonance of the tone. The nasal cavities are involved in resonance of tones, either as a focal point for sympathetic vibrations or as an area for resonance per se. They are also important to the quality of the voice—balanced or nasal. A warm and balanced tone will have resonance shaded by the vibration of tones through the nasal cavities.

The interior of the nose is comprised of two chambers separated by a straight wall or septum. The floor of the nose is the upper side of the hard and soft palate. The sides of the internal nose have turbinates which hang into the nasal cavity. These turbinates are able to expand and contract and have many mucous glands. When the air is dry the glands produce more mucus. Expansion or contraction of the turbinates changes the amount of mucus-producing area

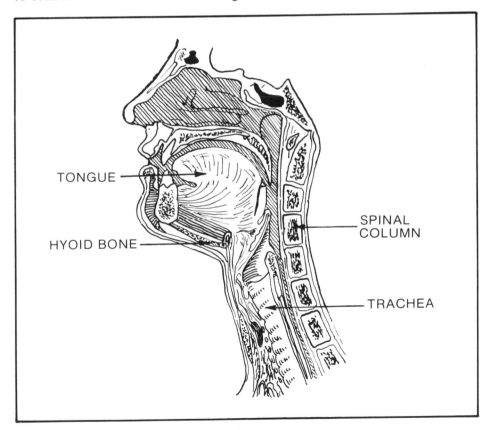

Figure 6a
The tongue and its relationship to the vocal tract

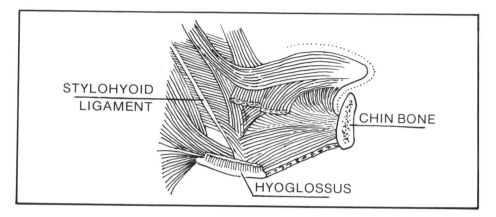

Figure 6b
Muscles of the tongue

depending on the quality of the air inhaled. If hurtful particles enter, the nose is capable of producing vast amounts of mucus. One cannot control any of this activity automatically, but it points out once again that the singer should avoid extremes of temperature when performing, and should avoid singing where there is danger of inhaling excessive dust, smoke, or other air pollutants.

There are many diseases which cause obstruction of the nose. Among these are allergy, polyps, deflection of the septum, and sinusitis. Any obstruction in the nose will alter the resonance. Many times, when one has surgery on the nose for "cosmetic" reasons, it affects the quality of the tone. A fine singer should think twice before having such surgery for cosmetic reasons alone.

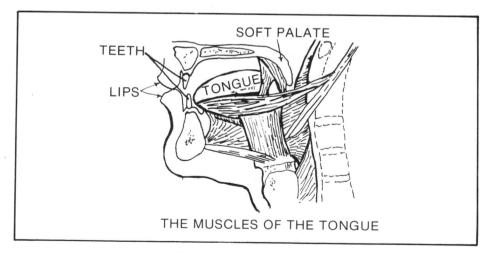

Figure 6c
Muscles connecting the tongue to other structures

THE ORAL CAVITY

The oral cavity is the entrance for food to the digestive tract. It begins with the lips and teeth. The hard and soft palate form the upper surface along with the upper teeth. The tongue and teeth dominate the lower portion. Behind the oral cavity is the oropharynx.

The tongue is a large muscle attached to the jaw and suspended from the hard palate by the muscles of the anterior and posterior pillars. The word "suspended" is most important. When one uses the inside smile, the tongue has a sense of freedom. It feels ready to jump into action in any direction the singer desires. In fact, this feeling, when properly attained, "makes you want to sing." When the inside smile is dropped, the tongue feels as if it has fallen into its bed for a bit of rest.

The tongue attaches underneath to the hyoid bone (Figures 6a, 6b, 6c). The hyoid bone is attached to the mandible or jaw bone, and to the skull, by muscles and ligaments. The larynx is suspended from this hyoid bone.

The many intricate muscles involved defy description in a book of this nature. The teacher of singing should obtain one or more of the excellent textbooks of anatomy. The greater one's knowledge, the greater one's understanding.

The tongue is interrelated directly and indirectly to the soft and hard palate, base of the skull, pharynx, larynx, and swallowing tube. Thus, the misuse of the tongue can change the vocal action in any of these areas, and result in a bad tone. The tongue aids greatly in the formation of words. If it is not properly aligned, the tongue can constrict the tone and make optimum resonance of the voice impossible. (Chapter 8 gives a detailed description of problems in singing that originate with the tongue as well as exercises to use to correct these problems.)

The teeth and hard palate are part of the oral cavity and are extremely important in the production of sound and its resonance, as well as being important in articulation. They also act as contact points for the tongue in the articulation of words, and especially consonants.

One of my students had diseased gums and was required to have parts of them cut away. She immediately lost her middle and low ranges because of the gaping holes between her teeth. She was fitted with an appliance to cover up the holes, and those parts of her range returned. The teeth must be strong, healthy, and in fine alignment. Fortunately the singer can (and must) seek good dental care throughout his singing career to preserve healthy teeth.

Another student came to me with quite a lovely singing voice but it sounded obstructed in some way. I could hear that it was coming from the oral cavity and I asked if she was wearing dentures. She was. I immediately called my son, a dentist, and he examined her. He stated that patients whose dentures are either ill-fitting or exceed their motor control to manage them—size, shape or distance between the upper gum ridge and the jaw—will find it difficult to have good diction. He also said that the size and placement of the front teeth in relationship to the lips is of great importance. He further explained that when a dentist fits a denture, he should be careful to add irregular ripples on the denture just behind the upper front teeth. These ripples tend to break up the air flow before it passes between the upper and lower front teeth and thus aid in forming certain consonants, vowels and diphthongs.

My son related to me that this student's denture was not fitting tightly enough and she was holding it in place with her cheek and jaw muscles, thus causing the strange sound in her singing and speaking.

Another student who came to me had caps or jackets on his front teeth. They seemed to cause a "thickening" or deadening sound as he was singing. My son told me that the construction of the caps is of critical importance for good diction. He explained that the more closely the caps imitate nature, the more likely the user will be to have good articulation. He emphasized that the surface toward the tongue must not be excessively thick, and natural-like ridges and grooves must be added to provide the tongue with a natural surface on which it can interact in a normal way to make sounds.

It is imperative that if a singer for any reason must have either dentures or caps or jackets made he find a dentist who knows the importance to his patient of the *careful* and precise technique which must be used to keep the tone natural, be it singing or speaking.

One can be born with an abnormality of the hard or soft palate or a condition can develop later. Attention by a physician or an orthodontist in childhood takes care of many of these problems. Common among the problems which affect the hard palate are nasal obstruction from allergy or enlarged adenoids. Early medical control with appropriate orthodontia usually results in a well aligned hard palate and good teeth. If the teacher of singing feels that there is some abnormality in the hard palate, it is wise to seek a medical opinion before launching the student on a professional singing career. This does not mean that the teacher should completely discourage a musical career.

THE PHARYNX

The pharynx is the common passageway for both air and food from the nose and mouth to the esophagus and larynx. The esophagus is a long tube leading to the stomach. The larynx or voice box is the opening for air to the

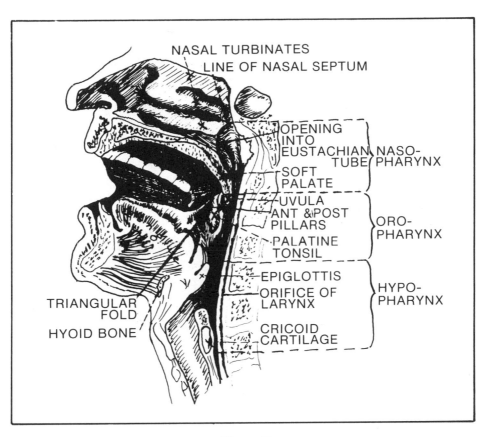

Figure 7
Pharynx: Nasopharynx, Oropharynx, Hypopharynx

lungs. The pharynx has three divisions: The nasopharynx, oropharynx, and hypopharynx (Figure 7).

The nasopharynx lies above the soft palate. As its name implies, the nasopharynx begins at the rear nasal openings. The nose has two chambers, the nasopharynx has one. The nasopharynx opens below into the oropharynx. The soft palate acts as a valve to open and close the nose and nasopharynx from the oral cavity and oropharynx. The soft palate is a muscular extension of the hard palate at the roof of the mouth. One can easily discern the end of the hard or bony palate and the beginning of the soft palate by passing the tongue or a finger along the roof of the mouth.

This muscular portion of the palate is of great importance in both eating and vocalizing. When one swallows, it closes off the nasopharynx and hence the nose.

During speech or singing, the soft palate determines how much air goes out through the nose or how much through the mouth. While humming or saying "mmmmm" the mouth remains completely closed. On the other hand, while saying "k," the air passes completely through the mouth. Thus, the action of the soft palate is of great importance to singing.

The oropharynx is the space between the soft palate and the epiglottis. The epiglottis is a flap-type valve which closes the larynx as food passes to the esophagus. The larynx is the opening to the lungs and thus must be protected during the passage of food.

The oropharynx therefore has three openings: the nasopharynx above, the oral cavity in front, and the hypopharynx below. The fauces separate the oral cavity from the oropharynx. The fauces have two folds on each side extending from the sides of the soft palate down to the tongue. Between these two folds lie the tonsils. The names of these two folds are the anterior and posterior pillars. These pillars contain muscles which interconnect the tongue with the soft palate. These muscles, with the help of the tongue, draw the palate down and close the oropharynx off from the oral cavity.

The soft palate, therefore, is closely related to the tongue. The tongue must always be readily and fully flexible. Any deviation in the performance of the tongue when singing or speaking prohibits maintaining a consistently beautiful tone quality.

The hypopharynx is the third and lowest portion of the pharynx (Figure 7). Its top is the upper edge of the epiglottis. The oropharynx empties into the hypopharynx. Another name for this area is the laryngopharynx because it lies directly behind the larynx. The esophagus or swallowing tube lies behind. The hypopharynx is the area in which the common food and air passage divides into the esophagus or food passage and into the larynx which is the entryway into the lungs. These two tubes share a common wall. The hypopharynx is directly behind the hyoid bone which, as mentioned earlier, suspends the larynx and in turn is connected by muscles and ligaments from the jaw, hard palate and skull. Once again, remember that this whole area "floats."

THE LARYNX

The larynx (or voice box) is behind the Adam's apple (Figure 8). The vocal cords are the most important structures within the larynx for it is here that the vocal sound begins. The vocal cords are sometimes called, perhaps more accurately, vocal folds. The edges of the folds are of a different texture than the rest of the fold, and that edge is what we call the vocal cords.

Healthy cords are white, and the rest of the fold is slightly pink. The vocal cords (Figure 9) are two firm bands of tissue which go from front to back.

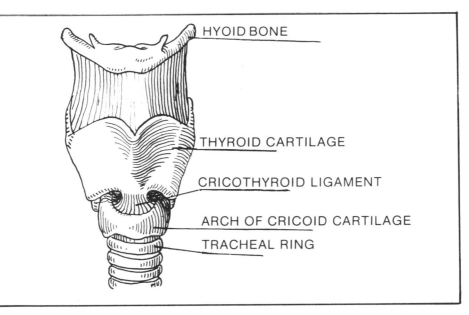

HYOID BONE

THYROID CARTILAGE

CRICOTHYROID LIGAMENT

ARCH OF CRICOID CARTILAGE

TRACHEAL RING

Figure 8
Larynx

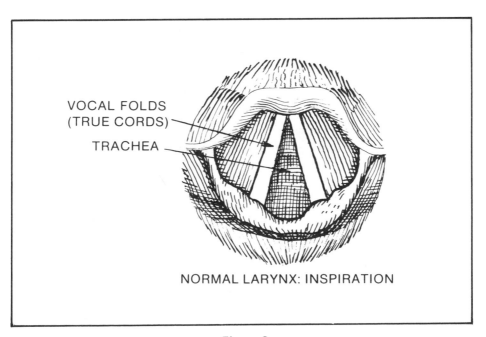

VOCAL FOLDS
(TRUE CORDS)

TRACHEA

NORMAL LARYNX: INSPIRATION

Figure 9
Vocal folds (inhalation)
(as seen from above in a mirror image)

When at rest they form a ''V'' shape with the top of the ''V'' at the front just behind the cartilage or gristle of the Adam's apple. Two pieces of cartilage covered with membrane constitute the back third of the cords. Between the open end of the ''V,'' muscles between the two pieces of cartilage bring the cords together. Muscles also attach to these cartilages to tense the vocal cords.

The Adam's apple has two cartilaginous structures. The one above is the larger of the two and is the thyroid cartilage. The cricoid cartilage lies below the thyroid; below that it attaches to the first cartilage of the trachea or breathing tube. Muscles lie between the thyroid and cricoid cartilages which, by contraction, can aid in tensing the vocal cords. Overuse of the voice can result in severe fatigue of any or all of these muscles with resultant bowing of the cords.

Above the vocal cords are the false vocal cords. In a normal voice, they do not contribute to the sound, but they contain many mucous glands and are therefore the ''lubricators'' of the larynx.

The involuntary nervous system controls the larynx. When light dims, the pupils of the eyes dilate. We do not have to learn this ability. This too is part of the involuntary nervous system and requires no conscious effort on our part. We must, however, decide whether to turn the light on or off. This action requires several voluntary actions and so we use the voluntary nervous system. We must first decide to get out of the chair, then which hand to use, which finger and so on. On the contrary, when the eye decides too much light is coming in, it simply closes the pupil without our thinking about it.

The larynx functions in the same way. All the singer must do is *think* the pitch he wishes to sing and the larynx, through the involuntary nervous system, takes care of the rest. It is absolutely true that we can *think* a tone where we want it to go. It will go there if it is not blocked by a tight jaw, or a pulled-back tongue or lack of breath support.

I hope that this lengthy discussion will emphasize the fact that any external manipulation of the larynx, whether by finger or any other device, impairs the function of the larynx and hence the quality of the tone. I will elaborate on this later.

THE LUNGS AND CHEST

The larynx is the opening into the lungs via the trachea or breathing tube. The trachea divides into two separate breathing tubes or bronchi as it progresses downward. The function of the two lungs, of course, is very complex since they take the oxygen from the air and exchange it for the carbon dioxide being expelled from the blood stream.

The singer should think of the chest as the cylinder in which a large piston (or diaphragm) moves up and down to move air in and out of the chest. The chest wall contains the ribs and spinal column. The ribs have muscles between them and are attached to the spine in such a way that the chest can be raised or lowered. The singer should think of his chest as the walls of a cylinder; the bigger the cylinder the better the singing engine.

THE DIAPHRAGM

The diaphragm is a great dome-shaped muscle that is attached to the sternum or breast bone in front, radiating around and under the lower ribs and then attached to the twelfth rib in the back (Figures 10, 11a and 11b). When the body is not properly aligned (rounded shoulders, swayed back, knees locked, tailbone out, etc.), the diaphragm is *not* in the best position in which to perform its functions in the breathing process. It must be properly situated so that it is able to operate maximally. The diaphragm functions as the major expiration and inspiration muscle by its ability to alter the volume of the thoracic cavity.

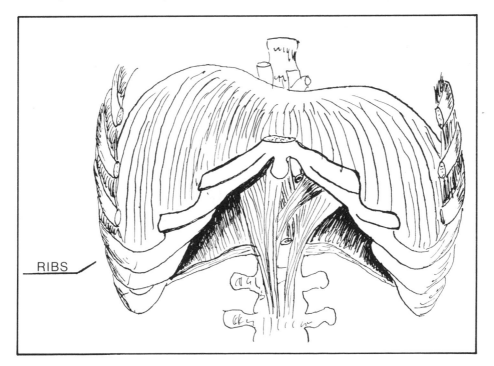

RIBS

Figure 10
Diaphragm

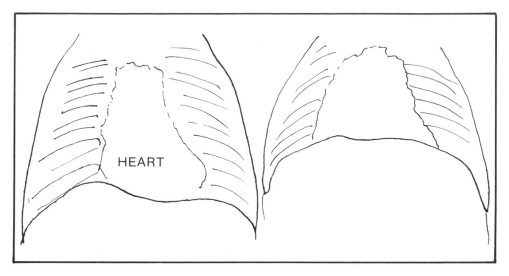

Figure 11a
Diaphragm (Inhalation)

Figure 11b
Diaphragm (Exhalation)

When the diaphragm descends, as in inspiration, it increases the volume of the thoracic cavity, lowering the intrathoracic pressure below atmospheric pressure and, hence, causes a flow of air into the lungs. When the diaphragm ascends, it increases the intrathoracic pressure above atmospheric pressure and pushes the air from the lungs through the mouth. Because of the necessity for increasing the volume of the thoracic cavity through the lowering of the diaphragm (and the reverse action of its ascent, decreasing the volume of the thoracic cavity), it is of utmost importance to give the diaphragm all the room possible for the action that I have just described.

The other parts of the anatomy related to the diaphragm and proper breathing are the lungs and abdominal area. The lungs and heart lie above the diaphragm while, from right to left immediately below, lie the liver, stomach and spleen, respectively. Because of this location of the stomach, it is almost impossible to sing one's best after having eaten a large meal. The diaphragm is unable to lower itself with a full stomach pressing upward.

Aside from the stomach and its effect upon the function of the diaphragm, the only important fact a singer should know about the use of the diaphragm is that it should be left alone. The singer should not interfere with its operation since most of its coordination is performed via the involuntary nervous system. *It takes care of itself if allowed optimal conditions for its functioning.*

When air is taken into the lungs, through the dropping action of the diaphragm, the abdominal muscles as well as the diaphragm itself are ready to control precisely the expiration of the available air. Through the use of exercises, the diaphragm and all the muscles associated with breathing (of which there are many) can be strengthened so that control of air as it is expelled is maximized. Such control allows for beautiful and resonant singing as well as for a steady vocal line.

KEY POINTS TO REMEMBER

1. The image of the voice ''sitting'' in a particular place is far preferable to thinking of ''placing'' the tone.
2. The muscles related to the nose are very important to correct singing.
3. The mask is especially important on bright vowels and aspirated consonants.
4. Every student and teacher should know the basic facts regarding the various parts of the pharynx and of the oral cavity.
5. One ''thinks'' the larynx into action since it is controlled by the involuntary nervous system.
6. A helpful image regarding breathing is that of a cylinder (chest) with a large piston (diaphragm) moving air in and out as a result of the involuntary nervous system.

4

HOW TO DEVELOP
CORRECT BODY ALIGNMENT
FOR VOCAL PRODUCTION

It is imperative for the student to begin immediately being conscious of body alignment. In this chapter, we shall discuss in detail the different areas of the body involved with correct body alignment.

WE SING WITH OUR WHOLE BODY

When a new student comes into my studio, be he a professional singer or just a novice, the lesson is begun by placing emphasis on the fundamentals, the most important being *correct body alignment.* Singing not only involves the vocal mechanism and facial area (the mask), but it also *must* involve the abdomen, chest area and the legs. We sing with our whole body!

The student's introduction to correct body alignment involves first learning correct body posture, and second, a series of exercises that will help him attain correct posture and maintain it while singing.

Correct body alignment begins with the placement of the singer's weight forward on the balls of the feet, *heels on the floor,* feet being best placed slightly askew, one somewhat in front of the other, and approximately four to nine inches apart depending upon the singer's height and weight (Figure 12). The tailbone is tucked or rolled under, causing the pelvis to shift forward. At the same time, this tucking action of the tailbone will automatically unlock the knees, allowing them to flex slightly. This position is *basic* to good control of the voice.

The flexed knee position is one of the most important factors in correct body alignment because this flexibility gives freedom in singing from low range to high range. Figure 13 illustrates the stiff, nonflexed knee position which is *not* compatible with good control of vocal sound production. Notice that the stiff knees throw the pelvis back pulling the abdomen with it. This position does not provide the lower abdominal area or the diaphragm with complete room for its proper action to take place. The knees must remain flexed so that there is a feeling of muscle flow from the toes through the entire body. The more advanced a singer, the more he is capable of singing without involving the legs (in lying and sitting postions, for example). But, from years of experience, I know that when a singer, advanced or beginning, begins to involve the legs, the tone becomes freer and fuller and the range of the voice widens. With increased development, the abdominal area and rib cage area eventually become so strong that the singer can sing in practically any position the stage director demands.

Figure 12
Correct body alignment
(knees flexed)

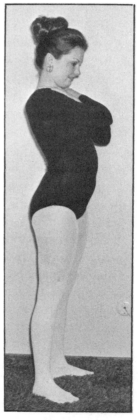

Figure 13
Incorrect body alignment
(stiff knees)

THE SHOULDERS, CHEST AND HEAD

As shown in Figure 14, the head and shoulders, as well as the chest area, are also an integral part of the most correct body alignment. The head remains level, the shoulders straight and the chest wide. Whether the singer is sitting or standing, this position will aid him tremendously in support of his tone.

There are usually many basic problems with most students when they first begin to concentrate on correct body alignment in the standing and sitting positions. Usually, their basic posture is wrong and needs immediate attention. Excluding the head positions, most body posture problems can be corrected by use of the exercises given below, if they are practiced daily. Rounded shoulders (Figure 15) which are positioned forward, almost always result in a "sunken chest," a position hindering good breathing technique and control.

THE EXERCISE FOR STRAIGHT SHOULDERS AND WIDE CHEST

Correct body alignment calls for straight shoulders and a wide chest. This alignment involves feet, legs, pelvic positions, etc., and it is basic to all the exercises given in this book. This postural position may not become a habit

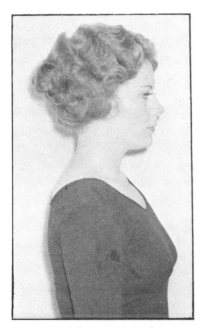

Figure 14
**Correct position of head
and shoulders**

Figure 15
**Rounded shoulders, sunken chest,
head and neck pulled forward (incorrect)**

Figure 16
Exercise position pulling shoulders back

immediately, but, through use of the following exercise, the singer will note a gradual and continuing improvement.

This exercise is begun by pulling the shoulders straight back (Figure 16) easily, not in a jerking motion, until the shoulder blades feel as though they are touching each other. The head and neck must be kept comparatively still and perpendicular to the ground as the shoulders are pulled back. This movement is completed four times, the last being modified by simply bringing the shoulders back and then pulling them down in such a fashion that the hands and arms reach for the ground. This exercise should produce a feeling of extreme width across the chest as well as a leveling of the shoulders. If this exercise is practiced every day, the defect of rounded shoulders will be alleviated and the chest widened. With these basic problems taken care of, the body will be provided a proper alignment conducive to greater control and maximum breath intake while singing.

THE SWAYBACK EXERCISE

Another problem fundamental to poor posture and greatly affecting correct body alignment in singing is the swayback (Figure 17) which causes an extremely high position of the chest and causes the knees to remain locked, throwing the pelvis and hips backward. The swayback can affect virtually all of the correct positions of the diaphragm, abdomen, knees, pelvis, hips, etc. The following exercise should be practiced every day to rid the singer of his swayback condition.

This exercise should be practiced on a corner wall that protrudes outward into space (Figure 18). The small of the back is placed against the wall by backing up to it slowly, standing straight and maintaining correct body alignment all the while. It is most important that the small of the back (note arrow), the middle part of the spinal column, be placed up against the corner. If it is difficult to do so, the feet should be allowed to move forward a few inches away from the wall. This should allow the small of the back easier placement against the corner. At this point, the back (entire spinal column) should be rolled up against the corner in a climbing fashion.

The pelvis should remain tucked under, the knees slightly flexed, so that the abdomen can spring forward. This action on the part of the abdomen facilitates lengthening and straightening of the spinal column as it lies against the corner. If practiced daily, the space seen between the wall and the spine will practically disappear. That space is what makes a back "swayed," and only concentrated and persistent efforts on the part of the singer through this exercise will help to overcome this problem of body alignment.

Figure 17
Swayback (incorrect)

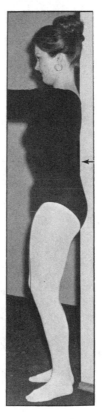

Figure 18
Exercise to eliminate sway back

THE HEAD POSITION

Some vocal problems can be corrected only by noting that the position of the head is limiting tone production. Singing with the chin held higher than is correct (Figure 19) and singing with the chin held lower than is correct (Figure 20) constricts the sound and does not allow for the most resonant, perfect tone to be produced. As shown in Figure 14, the best alignment for the head is that in which the head is held at a level position, with the tip of the nose pointing in a direction parallel to the ground. If, as in operatic staging, it is required that an aria (or a part of it) be sung with the head held high, pointing towards the balcony, or low, pointing towards the stage floor, the torso should slightly follow the head movement; *the head should not be moved solely from the neck.* This is not to say that the production of a song or aria is done rigidly with the head maintaining one position. The head can and should be moved around so as to create involvement and sustain contact with the audience while singing; but at the same time a level position should be maintained as the axis for that movement!

The reason head position is stressed here is because the neck, being part of head movement, has a muscular and skeletal physiology encompassing the spinal column, the larynx, vocal cords and tongue muscles (Figure 6c), all of

Figure 19   *Figure 20*
Chin pulled up (incorrect)   *Chin pressed down (incorrect)*

which are very close to each other. As we can see in Figure 6a, the spinal column is adjacent to the trachea which harbors the vocal cords. Any head movement to the extreme position away from the level position causes the spinal column to interfere with the air flow through the trachea and the production of sounds through the vocal cords.

Another problem related to the head being held too high or too low is that the tongue muscles tighten and pull or are pressed, resulting in abnormal and altered sound production. One way to effectively hear how head positions impair sound production is to talk with the head held high (Figure 19) and held low (Figure 20). As can easily be heard, and felt, it is very difficult to speak with the head in these positions. The sounds emitted are either constrained, inaudible, and/or muffled. It is much easier to sing as well as speak with the head held in the proximity of the most level position as illustrated in Figure 14.

TOTAL BODY COORDINATION

The total physique must be coordinated in singing just as it is in any sport. In golf, the player has a certain stance which he employs when preparing to hit the ball; likewise, the tennis player. An athlete hopes that by standing in this way, the ball will go exactly where he had wanted it to go.

Singing is very much like these sports. Many times when a golfer wants a ball to travel a great distance, he unwittingly uses what is termed a "muscled ball" which unfortunately drops the ball about half the distance he had intended. Such problems arise in singing. If a singer tries to "muscle a tone," it will not have as beautiful a quality and it will not carry as far. It will be a "forced" tone.

Through complete coordinated use of all the muscles involved in singing one can produce beautiful and resonant tones and maintain a consistent vocal line throughout the vocal performance.

KEY POINTS TO REMEMBER

1. We sing with our whole body—from head to toes!
2. Correct body alignment demands that:
    - the singer's weight be forward on the balls of the feet
    - the knees be flexed
    - the head remains level
    - the shoulders are straight, and
    - the chest is wide

5

DEVELOPING BREATH CONTROL
AND SUPPORT
TO INSURE WELL-PROJECTED VOCAL PRODUCTION

The most important of the foundations of singing is breath support and control. *All great singing demands complete breath control.* Building a voice is similar to the building of a house—the foundation must be solid and well-executed through perfect blueprinting with the aid of a knowledgeable architect. The foundations of a house must exhibit strength and endurance as must the foundations of a voice.

The first and most important technique used in building a good base for excellent singing is breath support and control. While working toward correct body alignment, this control and support can be initiated; *optimum support cannot be obtained without correct body alignment.* However, once the singer is secure in his singing posture, the breath support and control, so essential to the vocal line, can easily be acquired and maintained.

There are two factors which are basic to increasing this support and control. *The first factor is the study and practice of breathing exercises* which will indicate to the singer exactly where and how the different structures (e.g., abdominal area, diaphragm, thoracic cavity, lungs, mouth, etc.) are used together to assure proper breathing technique. Practicing these exercises will ultimately allow the correct breathing process to become second nature so that the singer never will need to think of breathing while singing.

The second factor is the actual physical exercise of the muscles involved in breathing. These physical exercises come from the daily practice of breathing exercises which strengthens the muscles from which breath support and control are initiated and maintained.

The singer should also consider some form of regular physical exercise (e.g., running, swimming, tennis, ballet) as a method to increase breath support and control. *I cannot stress this enough.* Strengthening the muscles used in singing and acquiring a feeling for just how they are coordinated during the breathing process are two extremely important factors in singing. Correct breathing technique should be learned and mastered for good vocal production and also to aid in resolving any vocal problems.

Many teachers of vocal technique support the theory that "natural breathing" is the only way in which the singer can obtain maximum results. This is true to only a limited extent. Singing requires a much more energetic tone than ordinary speaking and has a greater variety of pitch levels. With these demands and a wider range of dynamics and colors, singing must have greater support underneath the vocal line. Singers must unlearn many of the "natural breathing" misconceptions which they have been taught or otherwise acquired. These misconceptions are against the normal functioning of all the muscles involved in breathing.

Dr. Henry Hollinshead states, "Precise control of expiration as in singing *demands a particular degree* of coordination between the abdominal muscles and the diaphragm"[1] (emphasis added). Essentially, this medical text expounds upon the fact that control of breath in singing requires a more extended and advanced degree of coordination between the diaphragm and the abdominal muscles than in speaking. Singing, therefore, cannot be accomplished optimally by using a technique which requires only a "natural" breathing process, but it *can* be accomplished with a method involving a great degree of concentrated effort on coordinating the musculature basic to singing.

Most students of voice have no knowledge of their basic muscular and skeletal anatomy and physiology and are surprised to learn exactly where the diaphragm is located and how it functions. The manner in which the singer breathes and the way he uses his body in breathing mùst be learned.

"High" breathing, in which the chest is lifted, is an improper breathing technique for singers. Assuming that the chest is wide and the shoulders are level, the shoulders should not rise as air comes into the lungs. With continued study of breathing exercises, expansion ultimately will be felt in the lower rib cage and the back. The abdominal area visibly expands.

When the breath comes into the lungs, there should be no audible sound. This is accomplished by allowing the lower abdominal area to spring out. The diaphragm drops and the outside air pressure forces the air into the lungs. High

---

[1]W. Henry Hollinshead, *Textbook of Anatomy*, second edition, (New York, Harper & Row, 1967.)

breathing almost always constricts the tone by pulling on the laryngeal area, affecting all the anatomy involved in producing sung or spoken tones. Breathing with the best technique which I have described above will afford the singer the flexibility in singing long phrases as well as the ability to use a wide array of colors and dynamics.

VOCAL PROJECTION (VOLUME) IS THE RESULT OF CONSISTENT AND CONCENTRATED PRACTICE

Vocal projection (volume) should not be emphasized in the beginning of the study of voice. The more one builds the thoracic and abdominal areas and gains excellent breath control in the process, the more vocal projection will increase. The rate of increase of that projection is purely a matter of time and practice. The forte and piano tones will come eventually and should not be stressed at all. The volume grows as the control grows and as vocal technique is mastered. Through the vocal exercises given, the capacity of each singer will increase and control will be strengthened through practice.

Interestingly, many students who begin to study voice have a naturally fine tone and sing quite correctly. It is essential, therefore, to point out to such singers exactly why they sing correctly and then show them the exercises pertinent to continued correct singing. Reinforcement of correct technique through using these exercises, and explanation of why his natural technique is compatible with the exercises, will help the naturally gifted student maintain a good vocal sound. *Such vocal beauty can only be sustained when the gifted student knows exactly why he is singing well.*

VOCAL LINE AND ITS DEVELOPMENT

The vocal line is a difficult concept to understand and even more difficult to describe. It is based on sensations as they form vocal tones "riding" on controlled breath. The breath is controlled by the abdominal muscles and diaphragm. The vocal line is formed through the use of this controlled breath and a controlled technique which evens out each tone and makes each of the emitted sounds equal to each other in focus and resonance.

"Vocal line" is an evenness in the voice of a singer, and the beauty in a song comes when that line is steady and flowing. Breaking of the vocal line usually comes through improper breath support and/or an incorrect seat for the tones, causing the different ranges and perhaps "breaks" in the voice to become audible and well defined. The vocal line at its best forms one complete, well defined voice with no differentiation between ranges; it maintains a vibrancy and a total energy throughout the line. If the vocal line remains steady, then the text conveyed to the listener cannot be interrupted by faulty technique. An uneven vocal line alienates the listener from the composer's and librettist's original intent, both musically and literally.

The vocal cords initiate the tone through the involuntary nervous system, the thought of the tone being controlled by an impulse in the brain. Nothing should actually be felt in the area of the vocal cords; the cords and the whole laryngeal area should be free of any feeling. The sequence of sensations usually begins with the thought of the inside smile (Figure 3). Working with the inside smile eventually allows the muscles to involuntarily raise the soft palate, thus arching it. This action maintains an open back space which helps produce a warm, rich, and full tone. The movement of the jaw (easily swinging straight downward and up with the tongue lying wide and soft against the lower teeth) can be controlled through practice. The lips, of course, allow for the correct formation of the vowels and consonants sung throughout the line. Essentially, the vocal line is a feeling of an arch from the back of the throat upward over the soft palate, with an awareness that the well supported breath continues in a forward movement "taking that tone forward."

THREE VOCAL RANGES

The thought of tone does not originate with sensations, vibrations, or other physical actions, but rather with a nerve impulse from the brain indicating that a tone should be produced, and the pitch and feeling of that tone. In the *middle range* the thought of tone is directed into the cheek bones, each tone needing the wide open back space achieved by the inside smile. The strength of the middle range is sensed especially in the cheek area, while, the *higher* the tone, the more the tone feels as though it goes up through the top of the head

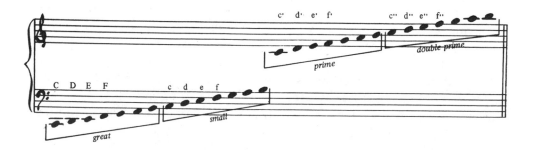

Figure 21

with practically no sensation. In the *lower range*, the thought of tone should be directed into the lower teeth, lower lip loose, the chest remaining wide and strong.

The jaw action in each of these ranges is an important factor in the ability of the tones to resonate properly and be properly "seated." The jaw moves very little in the middle range. In the case of the soprano, around d″ and e″ (notation indicated in Figure 21), the jaw should begin to swing further. Around b flat″ the jaw should swing even more in order to correctly "seat" the higher tones. The tenor will do this on notes an octave lower. For altos and basses, these notes could be a half to a full step lower than in the voices of their respective male or female counterparts.

The jaw also moves more in the lower ranges on such vowels as "ah," "oh," and "aw" (but always "in balance"—never too far), increasing in swing as the line descends. It is very important to sense where the note is in the vocal line and how the jaw is moving in relation to each of the ranges in order to keep the line steady and the tones equally resonated.

We know that there are two places where the vocal instrument makes an adjustment, but this is achieved by a brain impulse. I have found that when a student thinks of "registers" he will try to manipulate the laryngeal area. This is why I feel that it is best not to consider registers, but more appropriate to consider three *ranges*—low, middle, high. In this way, the techniques used to even out the vocal line are better served since technical principles can be more easily discussed in the context of three definitive ranges. There are certain principles which should be applied to each of the ranges; these principles involve *sensations* as well as *physical actions*. All of the sensations described above will eventually, through practice and a lot of "sensory perception" on the part of the singer, help to form an overall sense of the vocal line as well as maintain its steady and beautiful flow. The vocal line will then become stable and flowing and the act of singing will become instant, not a thought-out or consciously done process as it is in the beginning of studying vocal technique.

It is a good idea not to worry about these sensations and principles and best not to try to master them all at once. The more each exercise is practiced and the more each principle is drilled in and made an automatic process, the faster the overall, well defined vocal line will become second nature to performance. To think in a confused manner of everything at once (Where does the jaw swing on this note? What should be done with the tongue? The mask? How should they be employed when singing the "ay"? the "oo"? And the inside smile—how does it work; where is it?) will only serve to break down the slow block-by-block steps toward building a rapport between the neuromuscular system and the sensations we feel when we sing. Learn each concept one at a time via the exercises given in this text, practice them diligently, and the vocal line will become progressively steady and flowing.

KEY POINTS TO REMEMBER

1. The most important foundation of good singing is breath control and support.

2. "Natural" breathing must be modified for singing.

3. No audible sound should be made when inhaling.

4. A unified vocal line throughout the three vocal ranges is the major objective of vocal study.

5. Middle-range tones are directed into the cheeks, higher tones through the top of the head, and lower tones into the teeth.

6. The jaw swings very little in the middle range but more so on higher and lower pitches.

6

THE SEVEN BASIC EXERCISES
FOR DEVELOPING VOCAL ARTISTRY

In building anything, be it a voice, a car, or a house, one must always have the basic design for that structure. So it is with this technique; one begins with definite exercises to start building the framework for developing the voice. The following exercises are listed in the order in which they should be initiated. They each have their own definite purpose and must be practiced with great concentration. *Remember that all these exercises assume correct body alignment and the use of the inside smile as mandatory foundations.*

HŌŌK EXERCISE

Purpose

This is a beginning exercise to help get the breath moving; to strengthen the chest muscles and lower abdominal muscles; and to coordinate the muscles of the abdominal area and thorax.

Procedure

In order to feel the movement necessary in the "hook" exercise, one should first pull the lower abdominal muscles in rather *quickly* and *silently*, allowing the air in the lungs to be expelled through the lips which are slightly rounded. Now the lower abdominal muscles are released and the air should be allowed to come into the lungs. This should be repeated two or three times.

Now one hand should be placed just below the sternum and the other hand just above the pubic bone. The hands are placed in these positions *to emphasize the full extent of the involvement of the entire abdominal area,* the part of the body between the thorax and the pelvis (see Figure 22). Then, with a *whispered*

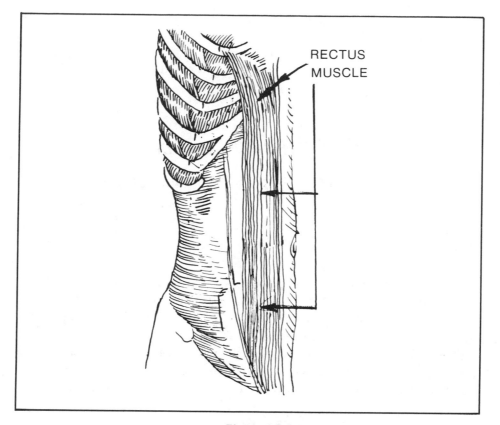

Figure 22
Abdominal muscles (side view)

"hoo" the abdomen should be pulled in, still allowing the air to be expelled through rounded lips. *It must be emphasized that the vowel in "hoo" is pronounced the same as the vowel in "moon."* At the end of the breath supply, a sharp (but not felt in the throat) voiceless "k" should be sounded which should cause a slight clutching of the muscles of the lower abdominal area just above the pubic bone. The lower abdominal area then pops out, the diaphragm drops, and the outside air pressure fills the lungs. This exercise is completed three times with a rest between each set of three.

Discussion

The reader should notice that, in the Procedure section, when discussing the action on the "k," I didn't say "plop"—I said "pop" out. When the lower abdominal area "plops" out, one has let all of that area loose and it is flabby. This is not what I want, nor do I want it held in, but there is a certain slight tautness across the lower abdomen when this exercise is correct.

If one feels width in the lower back rib area and does not allow the rib cage to drop, the lower abdominal area will have less tendency to "plop" out. There should be a feeling of leverage between the lower rib cage and the muscles across the lower abdomen just above the pubic bone. The late William Vennard, former Chairman of the Voice Department, School of Music, University of Southern California, explained, "This position of the ribs provides leverage for the action of the belly muscles. If the ribs collapse, the abdominal muscles cannot pull as effectively."[1]

If the rib cage goes in (collapses) as one is expelling the air, the muscles across the lower abdomen will not feel the correct coordination. When the lower abdominal muscles spring out, as mentioned earlier, the diaphragm drops and outside air fills the lungs. This is a readiness position to support a singing tone.

There are many muscles used in this exercise. As one pulls in the abdominal muscles expelling the breath, the chest should rise (the shoulders remain *quiet*). If the chest does not rise at first, one should not become alarmed. Generally speaking, this is a weak area of the torso, but one which is extremely important. By doing the "hook" exercise daily, the chest becomes stronger and will begin to move. The visible action—the combination of actions of all the muscles involved in the breathing process—is the action of the *abdomen,* the *chest,* and the *back ribs.*

The muscles eliciting the springing action of the abdomen can be lumped together and referred to as the "*hook muscle.*" When the singer or speaker uses the energy from the lower abdominal area (the "hook" or clutch) when dealing with consonants, he will experience no tightness in the throat or tongue area.

It is important to allow the throat to open wide as air comes into the lungs. If the lower abdominal muscles are held in rather than allowed to spring out as the air comes into the lungs, the breath will come only into the upper chest, causing the chest and shoulders to rise. This is incorrect coordination for good breath support and does not allow for complete control when vocalizing. The coordination of the diaphragm and the abdominal muscles controls the flow of breath and should be given maximum conditions under which it can perform. When the shoulders are high, the abdomen (and hence the diaphragm) cannot spring out to the fullest extent and therefore cannot effect proper control of the air when a tone is sung. The chest should be wide, but never pulled up.

It will usually take four to five instruction periods for the singer to acquire correct coordination and strength essential to this exercise. When the coordination of all the skeletal and muscular systems is finally attained, the act of

---

[1] William Vennard, *SINGING: the Mechanism and the Technic,* Revised Edition, (New York, Carl Fischer, Inc., 1967).

breathing while singing will be a natural function and one of complete support and control.

HEE-AH EXERCISE

Purpose

This exercise is used to initiate the movement of air and strengthen the abdominal and thoracic muscles. When it is performed regularly, control of the air and maintenance of the vocal line can be effortlessly achieved.

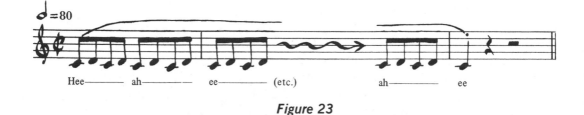

Hee———— ah———— ee———— (etc.)   ah———— ee

Figure 23

Procedure

This exercise should be preceded by two or three "hooks," whereupon one vocalizes *very lightly* "hee-ee, ee-ee, ah-ah, ah-ah." The exercise is sung in the low middle range of the voice as many times as possible on one breath *without allowing the chest to cave in,* at a moderate speed, and ending the sequence on "ee." The lower abdominal muscles should immediately spring out, and the singer should sing another "hee-ah" a half-tone higher.

Discussion

Initially, it is usually difficult to sing this exercise more than four or five times on one breath. One should always discontinue singing it before the chest caves in and shoulders drop forward. If one has difficulty letting the lower abdomen spring out at the end, it is best to whisper "hook" again and then try another string of "hee-ahs" for as long as possible. Through practice of this exercise every day, a gradual increase in the number of "hee-ahs" will be noted, and eventually a great increase in breath control and breath capacity will be realized.

When singing this exercise correctly, the singer should feel the abdomen move inward toward the spine and slightly upward toward the thoracic cavity. It is important to strengthen the musculature involved before trying to sing the "hee-ah" exercise fifteen to twenty times on one breath. As the chest and abdominal area become stronger, the control of expired air will come more easily.

Even though breathing is the most basic consideration given to this exercise, one should also be conscious of where the "ee" and "ah" sit. The employment of the mask, the inside smile, and the proper function of the jaw and tongue directly affect the performance of this exercise. If the tone is not far enough front on the "ee" and "ah" (particularly "ah") refer to the "preh" exercise (Figure 33). The student should feel the sensations of the "ee" and "ah" in the nasal "cavity" (but not singing a nasal sound).

The next consideration in singing the "hee-ah" exercise should be given to the jaw and tongue. The jaw should be allowed to swing very easily (without pressing it and not letting it drop too far) from the temples. It should drop from the width created under the eyes through the use of the activated mask. The width achieved through the mask area, caused by the inside smile, lifts the cushions under the eyes and creates a sensation of strength straight across the facial area. From this width, the jaw should swing freely like the jaw of a puppet—from the hinges, which are near the temples and in front of the ears, swinging *straight down* and *squarely*. The slight movement of the jaw begins on the "ah" after each "ee." The figure should be sung similar to "hee-ee-ee-ee" (swing), "ah-ah-ah-ah," and so on. As the jaw swings, the tongue should remain loose and wide with the tip against the lower teeth. *The jaw and tongue should move as one unit* without the tongue pulling back, grooving or bunching.

KEE-KAY AND KEE-KAH EXERCISES

Purpose

These two "k" exercises are sung as a unit and are used to strengthen the soft palate. When singing any word beginning with a "k," the fine muscles of the soft palate are automatically activated; the palate arches upward. This action, known as the "inside pull-up," opens up the space in the back of the mouth which gives greater space inside the mouth for resonance and formation of vocalized words. If these exercises are practiced every day, the soft palate will be strengthened. This will better facilitate a more even vibrato, better resonance and optimal conditions for eventual coloratura work.

Figure 24

Procedure

Each five-tone scale is always sung detached, and sung in the middle range, on one breath. The sequence should be practiced on "kee-kay" three or four times (each time a half step higher than before), then "kee-kah" three or four times in the same way.

Discussion

Always think the tone front. The last "kee" is sung staccato and quickly thrown away. (Students at first will have to be reminded many times "to get off the last pitch.") This is important because we are striving toward having the tone spinning up. When we sustain the last pitch, it has a tendency of pulling it down—not in pitch but in position.

The jaw and tongue action remain coordinated so that the tongue lies wide and soft against the lower front teeth *moving as a unit with the jaw* as it springs lightly on each aspiration of the "k." The inside smile facilitates phonation of the "ee" and "ah" and "seats" them in their most correct positions (tone front—back spaces open).

It is important to watch the action of the abdominal area as this exercise is sung. Body alignment (See Chapter 4) is important so that the action of the abdominal muscles can be complete and dynamic. As each tone of this five-tone exercise is sung, the abdomen should move inward towards the spine in a continuous and flowing fashion, the chest remaining wide and the abdomen springing out after the last tone.

If the lower abdomen is held in after the five tones are sung, the exercise should be discontinued and the "hook" exercise should be done before continuing. The "hook" will allow the correct action of the abdomen and chest to take over so that the "k" exercises can be performed with proper breath support. If the student does not allow the abdomen to spring out, he will "take a breath" and the shoulders will always rise—this is incorrect. The coordination of correct abdominal and chest actions with the act of singing takes time to master, but through practice, it will eventually become second nature.

FLAH-FLAH-NEE EXERCISE

Purpose

This exercise is used to obtain coordination between the tongue and the jaw. *The tongue and jaw should always move together.*

Figure 25

Procedure

The "flah-flah-nee" exercise is begun in the low middle range and is sung on one breath.

Discussion

It is important, first of all, that the "f" be sung correctly. The "flah" figure begins with the aspirant "f," which has a little puff of air after the initial light attack of the "f." This tiny puff of air is initiated between the lower lip and upper teeth, which should be placed together very gently, giving a good sensation of width across the chin and the mask. As the "f" is articulated, the upper lip should not be pulled down. The jaw swings, with the tongue and jaw moving as a unit, and the "f" is sung very fast.

The "l" and the "n" are simply formed by moving the jaw up and down, with the tip of the tongue lying wide and softly against the lower teeth. If the tongue does not move with the jaw (Figure 26), the tongue will tighten at the root and constrict the tone. When the coordination is correct, one feels the "l" and the "n" formed by the width of the tongue against the roof of the mouth while the tip rests gently against the lower front teeth. If the jaw shoots out on any part of the exercise (i.e., on either "flah" or "nee"), this changes the whole space of the oral cavity, and it pulls on the muscles in the back of the throat area which are connected down into the larynx. The jaw should always drop straight down in the back at the jaw hinge.

On the "flah" part of the exercise, a feeling of pulling up should be very strong in the upper lip but it should not be visible. (In other words, the upper lip should never pull down.) This will help to bring that tone front. If one does not have this feeling, the tone may be "flaw" instead of "flah."

A good method for sensing correct and incorrect movement of the tongue and jaw is by singing "lah-lah-lah-lah-lah" over and over. The *correct* way of singing this figure is accomplished by moving the tongue and jaw together so that the tongue lies wide and soft against the lower teeth throughout the movement. The jaw should swing very easily from the inside smile and not too far as the "lah" is sung, the jaw moving on each "lah." The jaw should move like that of a puppet, straight down. If the jaw is dropped too far, the mask will have a tendency to drop, and the vowels will not be sung as easily.

The *incorrect* way to sing the figure is to keep the jaw immobile and allow the tongue to form the "lah" figure by placing it behind the upper teeth (Figure 26).

Another precaution: when singing the syllable "nee," students sometimes pull the lower lip in over the lower teeth (Figure 27). This is incorrect. The lower lip should always be relaxed.

This exercise should employ the inside smile and the strong mask so that the vowel sounds will be given the best conditions in which they can be formed. If the jaw is dropped too far, the mask will have a tendency to drop and the "ah" and "ee" will not be sung as easily.

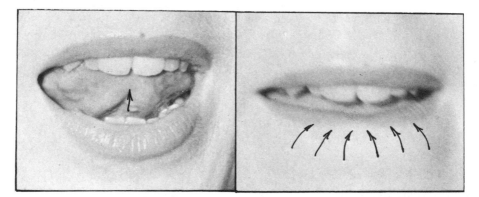

Figure 26
Tip of tongue pulled up
on "l" and "n" (incorrect)

Figure 27
Nee, lower lip pulled in
(incorrect)

NING-EE AND NING-AH EXERCISES

Purpose

These exercises help the singer to acquire facility in focusing vowel sounds by bringing the sound forward.

Procedure

Be sure the jaw feels loose in the hinge and that it does not remain immobile so that the tongue is doing all of the work. (This is often a problem, especially with the "ning-ee.") This exercise is sung in the middle range on one breath and is sung legato. Each of the two should be practiced three to four times, each time ascending one-half step. Don't forget the inside smile!

Ning--ee - - ning - - ee - - - ning - -ee - - - - ning - - ee - - - - - ning - - - ee
Ning--ah - - ning - - ah - - - ning - -ah - - - -ning - - -ah - - - - - -ning - - - ah

Figure 28

Discussion

Be sure that the jaw is swinging *slightly* on the "ah" and not being held stiff. The "ning-ee" and "ning-ah" *automatically* bring focus into the tone. Don't press the tone, and don't try to "focus" since the "ning" automatically does this for you. One usually feels a vibration in the bridge of the nose when that focus is there.

NG EXERCISE

Purpose

This exercise is excellent for extending both the lower and upper ranges, and helps to bring the tones forward and to focus them. It also bridges the voice over from one range to another.

Figure 29

Figure 30

Figure 31

Procedure

The learning of this exercise is begun by *speaking* the word "hung." The "ng" should be lengthened as though humming it. This allows the tone to "sit" in the proper area of the mask and indicates just where the sensations of the "ng" exercise will be based. Another method of sensing where the "ng" sound will originate is simply by producing the sound "ng" on the tone sequence 5-4-3-2-1, legato (Figure 29). If the tone is "sitting" far enough front, the legato comes easily. If it is too far back it "bumps" down the back of the throat. Sometimes whining through the nose like a little puppy dog, allowing the jaw to swing up and down freely, will assist in finding the "ng" spot.

Upon having sensed the "ng" in the correct spot, the exercise is begun by singing "ng" on the tone shown in Figure 30. The exercise is sung in one breath in the middle range and is sung very legato (no "stair-stepping" effect) with each tone articulated but "arching over" to the other. (Note, I said "arching," not *slurring* one tone into the other.) The entire exercise should be sung three to four times, each time a half step higher than before.

After singing the "ng" exercise as described above, the "ng" is sung again, to a one octave descending scale (Figure 31). Each succeeding octave is sung one-half step higher than the one before it, inhaling between each octave. The sequence is sung with each tone connected and arching into the other. The jaw should swing on the first tone and should remain down (but not held down) throughout the remaining tones. When the sequence is at that point in the high range where it is relatively easy to do so, the octave figure is extended to two octaves (and sometimes three). The exercise should be taken as high as is comfortable, always feeling that the voice could go at least one-half step higher. This more advanced version should be attempted only when the basic "ng" has been mastered.

Discussion

The sensations are very evident in this exercise because of the great involvement of the nasopharynx and the hard palate, particularly in the middle and low range. The sounds "sit" very far forward on the front part of the hard palate. If the student has difficulty sensing the "ng" in this area of the nasopharynx, he should precede the "ng" sound with a slight puff of air outwards through the nose before the tone starts.

This tone has a sensation of being in the nasal cavity. Lest you fear that this exercise will produce a nasal voice, hold your nose closed and try to make an "ng" sound. No sound comes forth. This illustrates that we sing *through* the nose and that the nasopharynx is a very vital area of singing. The sound is similar to that of a hum.

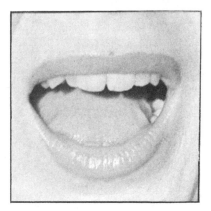

Figure 32
Correct position of mouth and tongue
while singing "ng" exercise

The inside smile should be present throughout the exercise. The tongue should follow the jaw and remain wide and soft against the bottom teeth (Figure 32).

The "ng" exercise should be practiced with care and the tones should not be forced. They should come easily, and restraint should be used in trying to take the octave figure up higher than is comfortable to sing. The "ng" attack on the first tone should never be glottal (initiated by banging the vocal cords together) but should be sung on the air as it passes from the trachea as the jaw springs lightly (never forced down or pressed).

When one is extending the range with the "ng" and the first pitch of the two octave scale does not come easily but has a tendency to stick, the breath flow should be started through the nasal cavity before starting the actual sound. *Be sure the jaw swings at the start.* Be sure the mask is wide and the lower abdomen is involved. Let the tone go straight up through the top of the head.

Another way to get the higher pitch to come easily is to gently lay the tongue out on the lower lip while singing the "ng." Sometimes it is impossible for the singer or the teacher to detect any pressure or tightness in the back of the tongue, but when the student lays the tongue out loosely on the lower lip, the pitch will go up easily into the top of the head. By doing this exercise in this manner, one increases the space of the whole pharyngeal area.

PREH EXERCISE

Purpose

It will open up the spaces of the nasal cavity, giving resonance to the short vowels.

Preh   preh   preh   preh   preh
Prih   prih   prih   prih   prih
Pra   pra   pra   pra   pra
Pruh   pruh   pruh   pruh   pruh

Figure 33

Procedure

This exercise is always sung the same way with deviations only in that different vowel sounds are used. The exercise is sung very easily (never full-voiced) in the middle range in one breath, with one of the figures (for example, "preh") sung on each of the five tones as they descend; each tone should be detached. It should be sung on "preh," "prih," "pruh," and "pra."

The upper lip is consciously pulled up as the "p" is sung with the flipped "r" (Figure 34). The sensation is localized around the nostrils and upper lip *without wrinkling the bridge of the nose* (Figure 35). Each succeeding repeti-

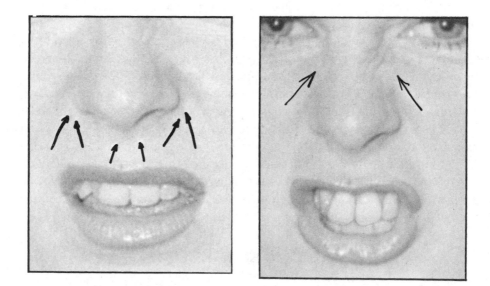

Figure 34
Correct position of lips
while singing "preh" exercise

Figure 35
Nose wrinkled while singing "preh" exercise
(incorrect)

tion of the figure should be one-half step higher than the one before; every two or three times that it is vocalized a new vowel sound should be introduced.

Discussion

If done correctly, a sensation of warmth will be felt on the upper lip and in the area around the flanges of the nose.

The activation of the pulled-up lip is extremely important in getting the English short vowels to "sit" properly in the nasal cavity. After the upper lip muscles are strong, one never sees the action from the outside but one always feels its assistance while singing.

Although many of the exercises in this technique are involved with the musculature of the face, one will be left with a normal, pleasant expression on the face—never distorted to get consonant or vowel sounds. You should never sing as if you are doing facial gymnastics.

****

The above exercises plus the introduction to correct body alignment and correct breath control and support are basic techniques used to acquire a good and solid vocal line. If the exercises are practiced consistently, making sure that each principle is understood, the voice will improve in quality, tone, size and texture.

The basics of good sound production have been given: correct body alignment, proper breath control, the parts of the body essential in correct production of vowels and consonants, and the basic exercises used to obtain all of the correct coordination.

The first few lessons usually employ all of these, and the singer should try to practice them with concentration every day. With this concentration, he will learn to couple the basics with newer, more advanced exercises, allowing him to become totally familiar with the correct coordination of all systems involved in singing correctly.

Each principle learned and illustrated in each of the exercises should be employed when introducing new and more advanced exercises (Chapter 7). I never abandon the basic exercises, although I shorten the time that I use them as I add the more advanced exercises. The principles of the exercises should also be applied to the singing of words written in vocal texts.

At times the instructor will wish to interject corrective exercises (Chapter 8) to deal with specific vocal problems and to help perfect the production of the present exercises. Many of these corrective exercises will help to increase breath support and aid in the correction of basic problems such as the shaking jaw, bunched tongue, and sunken chest. These exercises are described on a somewhat more advanced level and should be employed only after the basic exercises have been mastered by the singer. Adding too many exercises (basic, accelerated and/or corrective) at one time may only add to the student's confusion and will most probably be detrimental to his learning process.

As the instructor studies and uses these exercises, he will develop an instinctive knowledge, a sense of timing as to when new and/or more difficult exercises should be given.

7

ADVANCED EXERCISES
FOR DEVELOPING THE VOICE
TO ITS FULLEST POTENTIAL

As the student masters the seven basic exercises (Chapter 6), new exercises should be added. Most of the exercises given in this chapter should be used when those in Chapter 6 have been somewhat perfected, since the use of the more advanced exercises will tend to amplify the principles basic to the more elementary exercises. At the beginning of lessons and practice time, one should *always* begin with the basic exercises *before* going on to the advanced ones.

Some of the exercises described here are variations on the basic exercises, expanded and/or elaborated upon. Others involve totally new concepts. *These exercises involve principles which can be applied to the singing of vocal literature and will help to impress upon the student exactly how and why the principles basic to them work when singing vocal literature.*

HOOK EXERCISE (VARIATION)

Purpose

It will help the singer to get complete feeling of the whole thoracic cavity being involved.

Procedure

The variation of the ''hook'' exercise given here is very simple. Three ''hooks'' are whispered with sharp ''k's'' after the ''hoo'' sound (the ''k'' placed via the lower abdominal muscles and not via the throat). The abdomen springs out with the pronunciation of the ''k,'' the chest remaining wide. The fourth "hoo" is also whispered quickly, but then the breath is suspended for five counts, the "k" is added sharply at the end of the count and the abdomen springs out.

Discussion

All the points regarding the use of the abdominal muscles, chest, etc., outlined in the discussion of the basic "hook" exercise are valid for this variation.

HAWK EXERCISE

Purpose

This exercise helps the singer to experience great support from the abdominal area as a result of the vocalization of the syllable.

Figure 36a   Figure 36b

Procedure

The "hook" is always whispered and the "hawk" is always voiced. The "h" is an aspirant and one should feel it pulling the lower abdominal muscles before the tone is sounded. As the "h" is pronounced, one has the same feeling of a slight clutching of muscles above the pubic bone, as one feels when pronouncing the "k" on the "hook" exercise. When singing the skip of the fifth, one should be sure that his jaw swings downward.

CIRCLE–ARM BREATH EXERCISE

Purpose

It will increase breath capacity and help control expiration of air.

Procedure

The exercise is performed using correct body alignment (Figure 12), with the tailbone under, knees flexed, chest wide, shoulders straight and the body weight placed forward on the balls of the feet. As shown in Figure 37, one arm should be placed behind the back, high and between the shoulder blades with the palm of the hand turned outward. In this position, the chest will pull across from shoulder to shoulder and give a great feeling of width and strength across the chest area. When the breath is taken in and let out, the arm behind the back will sense the steady movement of all the muscles involved.

The other arm circles closely in front of the body, very slowly, with the wrist leading toward the direction of the first arm (Figure 38). As the arm circles, the air should be inhaled very slowly through the teeth until the circling arm has reached a position straight above the head, perpendicular to the ground (Figure 39). During this half of the circle, the thoracic cavity expands and the lungs gradually fill with air. During this inhalation, the abdomen should gradually move outward.

Once the circling arm is positioned over the head, a stop should be made for a few seconds and the arm should then continue the circle back downward (Figure 40). As the arm comes down, the air should be exhaled very slowly and steadily, through the teeth, with great control of the abdominal (moving inward) and rib cage areas; about three-fourths of the air is expelled. Then, the remaining air should be forced out through the teeth with strength from the lower abdominal area, creating a strong "ssh" sound. The chest should not be allowed to collapse.

The abdominal area moves inward as the air is exhaled. As the abdomen is released, air should be allowed to rush into the back ribs as quickly as possible.

As the abdomen springs out, the air should be allowed to rush into the lungs, thus expanding the thoracic cavity, particularly the back of the rib cage. The breath is taken in through the nose and mouth and not through the teeth. At this point, the circling arm should be positioned straight downward and again perpendicular to the ground while the other arm remains positioned behind the back.

The exercise is then repeated, reversing the two arms.

Discussion

The correct coordination of this exercise is difficult to master in a short time and should be attempted only after the basic breathing exercises ("hook" and "hee-ah") have been learned properly (probably after eight or ten lessons). As this exercise is worked on, breath capacity and support will be increased, and practicing it will help to develop the involved muscles and integrate their actions with those of the legs and torso.

As the air is exhaled, the entire body will feel a total energetic, muscular sensation as the chest remains wide and the abdomen moves inward. The legs

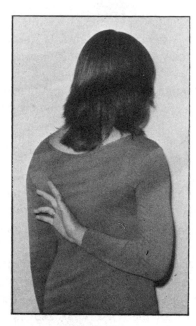

Figure 37
Preparation for circle-arm breath
(back view)

Figure 38
Arm crossing in front of body
during inhalation of circle-arm breath

Figure 39
Position between inhalation and exhalation
during circle-arm breath

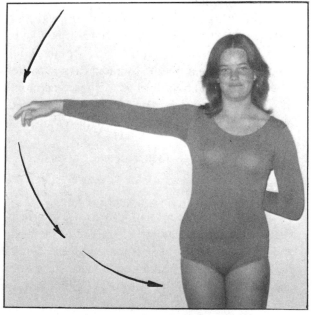

Figure 40
Arm coming down during exhalation
of circle-arm breath

and torso are basic to support in singing and are important sensory grounds for the muscular energy. If any of the muscular systems involved in singing collapse while controlling the air, the vocal line will be disturbed, and it will be almost impossible to have good coloring and phrasing.

S-S-S BREATH EXERCISE

Purpose

The ''s-s-s'' aids in developing the ability to sing long phrases.

Procedure

As with all the exercises, one must start with proper body alignment. The ''ss'' sound is a hissing sound made through the teeth. This sound is made very lightly with the tongue lightly touching the roof of the mouth.

For the first ''s'' a breath is taken in through the mouth and nose and the ''ss'' sound is made while exhaling air slowly. Breath is allowed to rush into the lungs (again through the mouth and nose, without grabbing or sucking in the air) by allowing the abdomen to spring out between the first and second hissing sound and the second and third hissing sound.

Discussion

It is important that the facial area remain strong and wide, the cushions lifted slightly during the production of the ''ss'' sound and during the intake of air, all the while using the inside smile.

When the ''s-s-s'' exercise is performed correctly, the breath is taken in quickly (in a snap-like fashion) through the mouth and nose. The lungs will automatically fill with air and the diaphragm will naturally drop (as described in Chapter 6). The chest area should remain strong and wide without any uplifting motion of the ribcage as it expands. When the snap-like breath is taken in, the abdominal area should spring out naturally and should not be held in purposely.

As the ''ss'' sound is made, the abdominal area should move slowly inward towards the spinal column until all of the air is exhaled. When the air is expelled slowly in this way, the musculature involved in breathing will be exercised, and, over a period of time, breath control and support will be increased as the muscles are strengthened. The air flow should be even during the inhaling and exhaling.

BACK BREATH EXERCISE

Purpose

This exercise is used to develop an expansive and strong ribcage which will easily contract and expand when necessary for taking in air and expelling it while singing. It is impossible to pick out one specific muscle used in the breathing process and state that through a given exercise *that* specific muscle will be exercised. Yet, the many muscles strengthened through practice of this exercise are those of the back, stomach, and thoracic cavity, all of which act to control the expansion and contraction of the ribcage.

Procedure

The back breath exercise is begun by bending over and placing the arms (folded) on the top of a piano, or on something at about the same height (approximately 4 feet). The head should be placed on the folded arms so as not to hamper the intake and expelling of air. The torso should be almost parallel to the floor, the back straight and the knees slightly flexed. A full, snap breath is then taken in, with the abdomen springing outward, away from the spinal column. The lungs will fill with air automatically when the abdomen springs out, and the diaphragm will lower itself to its active position.

When the lungs are filled, the air is then slowly expelled *through the teeth* in a sound of "sh" (similar to a long "hushing" sound) until every bit of air is exhaled. As the air is exhaled, the abdominal area should move slowly inward towards the spinal column, the back remaining strong and wide. When all the air is exhaled, another snap breath is taken so that the lungs quickly fill with air. A strong sensation of width and pulling should be felt across the back and through the ribcage.

The exercise is completed three times with a snap breath between the first and second "sh" sounds and the second and third "sh" sounds. After the final exhalation of air, a final snap breath is taken in order to expand the ribcage and back area a fourth time; the air is simply exhaled in one muscular movement without the "sh-sh-sh" sound.

Discussion

When the above exercise, coupled with the other breath exercises, is practiced daily, the process of breathing while singing will become an effortless action on the part of the singer. There will be no audible breath and no visible strain (or even very little motion at all). Once the ribcage is strengthened, the chest remains stable and the back remains strong and wide. It is important to practice the breathing exercises, but, when one begins to sing, the concentration must *not* be on holding the ribs wide. The concentration should be on the lower abdominal muscles where the strength for the "hook" and "hawk" are felt.

BALLET STRETCH

Purpose

This exercise will stretch the ribcage to give more space for rib expansion.

Procedure

One arm is curved in front of the body and the other arm arched over the head in the opposite direction, both arms pulling as one bends sideways, stretching the entire side of the body of the arm that is arched over the head. This exercise should be done on both sides, reversing the arms. The stretching should always be done slowly—never jerkily.

KAH-KAY-KEE-KOH-KOO EXERCISE

Purpose

This exercise is related to the "k" exercises which are described in Chapter 6 and should not be attempted until after those have been mastered. These "k" exercises strengthen the soft palate and the muscles connecting to it, allowing for greater flexibility and increasing the ability to ornament.

Figure 41

Procedure

This exercise is sung detached and in one breath. A breath should be taken between the ascending and descending tone sequences. The exercise is vocalized at a moderate rate of speed when first attempted but, after practice, the rate at which it will eventually be sung will be quite fast. The exercise should never be sung more than three or four times (always ascending one-half step each time).

Discussion

The soft palate is one of the most important structures of the pharyngeal area in the "seating" of tone, the shimmer of that tone, and the control of a flexible and easily moving line.

All of the basic concepts, such as the inside smile and pull-ups, the employment of the mask, and the swing of the jaw on the beginning of the consonant "k" should be applied to this exercise. Use of these concepts brings tones forward into their correct positions and therefore helps to focus the vowels. The "k" placed before each of the vowel sounds automatically starts the lifting action of the soft palate. The back space needs to be very open so that the consonants and vowels can be more easily sung. These wide back open spaces help to keep present the arch which is so important to proper formation of the resulting vowel sounds.

The jaw and its movement play another important role in this exercise. It must be loose and spring very lightly on each syllable, but it should not be dropped too far—only slightly. Most of the action on each of the sounds is done inside the mouth with the big wide space in the back and the connection of the tongue against the soft and hard palate as the "k" is produced, *thinking the tones front*.

It is usual, when beginning the practicing of this exercise, for the "kay" and "kee" to stick (the tone will not phonate). If it does stick, it is best to wait a few weeks until the soft palate is stronger. If practiced each day over a period of time, the soft palate will become strengthened.

KEE-KAH-KEE EXERCISE

Purpose

The "kee-kah-kee" exercise is another "k" exercise used to strengthen the soft palate and to develop the inside arch. It also helps to illustrate the action of the jaw and the position of the tongue as the jaw swings lightly. The swinging action of the jaw with the tongue is emphasized in this exercise as well as the employment of the inside smile and the strong, wide mask. It is important that the tones be sung "front."

Procedure

The entire sequence is sung in one breath in the middle range. The first

Figure 42

half is sung detached, with the jaw swinging on each tone, while the descending figure is sung legato on the "ee" and "ah" with each tone connected. The entire exercise is sung not more than four times, each time one-half step higher than the preceding one.

Discussion

All the advanced "k" exercises should not be used at one time. In each daily sequence one should be chosen and used, but never all in one exercise sequence. The tongue position in the "k" exercise should be forward, wide, and softly placed behind the lower teeth. Be sure the tongue and jaw move together.

The "k" exercises in this chapter will help to eliminate the pressed tongue problem (See Chapter 8) if practiced thinking "wide soft tongue" and with concentration.

KOO EXERCISES

Purpose

These "koo" exercises are particularly beneficial in helping to develop the "head voice." They also are most beneficial in helping to develop the trill.

Figure 43

Koo   koo   koo koo koo   koo   koo ——————

Figure 44

Procedure

The jaw should move loosely at the back but not too much. The lips are *slightly* rounded (Figure 45), not tight, and one feels the ''oo'' going up through the hard and soft palate. The tongue is lying front, wide, and loose as the descending ''oo'' scale of Figure 43 is sustained.

Discussion

The soft palate must be very supple in order for one to sing a good trill. The ''koo'' exercises are invaluable in developing this soft palate area. They *allow* the trill to go into the spaces where the tones move more easily. The jaw

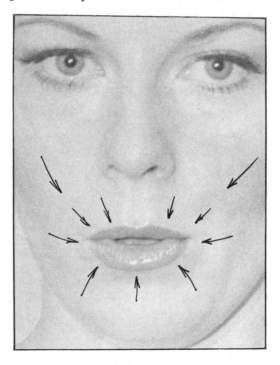

Figure 45
Rounded lips while singing ''oo''

moves loosely at the hinge, the inside smile is present, and lips are slightly rounded; this prepares the singer for an easy trill. The trill must have back space behind it and feel as though it goes straight up to the top of the head. If a tone catches in the nose, a trill is impossible.

FLAH-FLAH-NING-AH EXERCISE

Purpose

This exercise is a development of the "flah-flah-nee" exercise described in Chapter 6, and is used for a more advanced study of focus, and correct jaw and tongue action.

Figure 46

Procedure

The "flah-flah" portion of the exercise is performed as in the "flah-flah-nee." The "ning-ah" portion of the exercise is sung as described in the "ning-ah" exercise (Figure 28) with the "ning" being very far forward, buzzing across the bridge of the nose. The "nee-nay-nee-nay-nee" figure involves a great deal of action with the jaw; the vowels are again formed by employment of the inside smile and the inside and outside pull-ups. The jaw swings lightly with the tongue following it lying wide and soft against the lower teeth.

Discussion

The interval on which "ning-ah" is sung involves the most spring of the jaw: "ning" (jaw swings down on the "n" and then up for the "-ing"); "ah" (jaw swings down again lightly). The "nee-nay-nee-nay-nee" should be sung with a very wide open back space initiated through the employment of the inside smile, but one should always be careful not to swing the jaw too far.

RAG DOLL EXERCISE

Purpose

This exercise helps the singer to get rid of tension.

Procedure

The body drops from the waist towards the floor very limply, allowing the head to drop. The neck should not be stiff, and the knees must not be locked.

Discussion

The "rag doll" exercise completely releases all the tensions in the body. One feels as if the spine is unraveling. The "wide snuff" exercise (see following) can be done in this position.

WIDE-SNUFF EXERCISE

Purpose

This exercise is used to open the nasal cavity and the whole pharyngeal area, and to eliminate laryngeal tension.

Procedure

The cushions under the eyes are consciously pulled up, the jaw drops loosely (but not too far) at the hinge, not disturbing the cushions under the eyes. The tip of the tongue is front, against the lower front teeth. The back of the tongue is up, against the roof of the mouth. Inhale *slowly* through the nose (the flanges of the nose will always widen). Be sure not to involve the muscles of the neck on inhalation. It is a *gentle* inhalation. Now lower the tongue to a wide position and exhale through the mouth *slowly* and *silently*. (Figure 47).

Discussion

This exercise opens the nasopharynx in the inhalation, and the complete throat on the exhalation, the soft palate lifting very gently during the exhalation. This exercise can be very beneficial in preventing any tightness coming into the tone as one begins working with the upper range. The wide snuff can be done standing in an erect position, as well as in the rag doll position. *Thinking* of the sensations of the wide snuff before singing any high pitch will help the pitch to be easily sung.

If using the wide snuff in conjunction with the rag doll (see above), one should do a complete wide snuff and then do again the first half of the wide snuff (the inhalation) then come back easily to an erect position to sing the high note. This is especially beneficial when working on the high descending "ng" scale. This sequence makes one aware of the width of the back rib cage, the space over the soft palate, and the strength under the eyes. The exaggerated mask width used in the wide snuff should not carry over into normal singing situations, since the audience should never be aware of a "technical" look on the outside of the face. The singer should, of course, be aware of

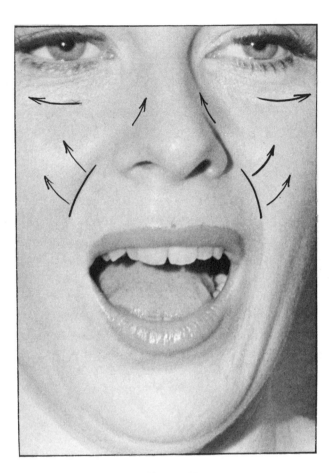

Figure 47
Face position for wide snuff

the inside sensations of the wide snuff. Regular use of the wide snuff with the "ng" exercise can enable many singers to descend three octaves or more with ease and with no break in the vocal line. This goal should not apply to everyone and is not imperative. After reaching the top of the range, immediately go to an exercise for the low range (see below). (It is important *not* to come back down from the upper range in half steps. The voice will stay in balance if you go directly into the low range.)

HEE-AH AND HAH-AH EXERCISES

Purpose

These exercises help the singer to develop the lower range.

Procedure

One should start the first syllable with a heady tone (feeling as though he is sighing), allowing the jaw to swing into the bottom note, making a cre-

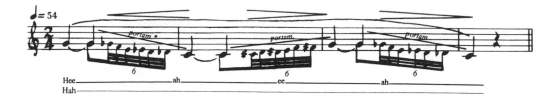

Figure 48

Future portamenti used in these exercises are to be sung in similar fashion; occurring on the "final eighth note" of the preceding note.

scendo. The jaw swings back to its original position, returning to the top note on a decrescendo, and then back to the bottom note with another jaw swing (with no crescendo).

Discussion

The swinging of the jaw, thinking head voice into the tone, will keep the tone from going into a raw chest tone. As one descends to the bottom note, he should think the tone into the hard palate area and lower teeth, also thinking of the sternum coming up under the tone for support.

WAW-EE

Purpose

This exercise helps the singer to develop the lower range.

Figure 49

Procedure

Before attempting the exercise, one should do the first half of the wide snuff and say "waw." The mask is not involved per se: it is not dropped, but neither is it as wide as on "ah." When one says the "ee," the jaw swings up (as it would normally when an ''ee'' is said), and the mask is immediately involved.

This exercise is begun on middle C and one goes down as low as is comfortable, always being certain that the ''waw'' has the big wide snuff sensation before starting it. Otherwise, it will be a raw chest tone and the scale will not ascend easily. The ''aw'' sound feels as though it goes back up over the soft palate. On the decrescendo, the tone should be arched forward, with the back spaces open. The tone should never be pressed down.

Discussion

This exercise outlines the complete gamut of vowels from ''aw,'' the vowel that goes back farthest in the oropharynx area to, ''ee,'' the brightest and most forward.

This exercise also can be used to help the middle range by singing ''waw-ee-ah,'' allowing the jaw to swing *slightly* on ''ah'' from the ''ee'' position. One feels a great deal of strength through the mask and over the hard and soft palate, as though the roof of the mouth is being pushed up (not drastically, but with a definite sensation of upwardness).

If the vibrato is not even in this exercise at first, the student should do a ''ballet stretch,'' keeping the back rib cage involved through the whole exercise. If the vibrato is too uneven, discontinue the exercise until the body and the inside pull-ups are stronger.

NG-EE-AY-AH

Purpose

This exercise enables the singer to get focus into the ''ay'' and ''ah.''

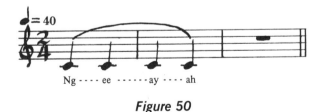

Figure 50

Procedure

The jaw should come up on the ''ee,'' retaining the inside position of the oral cavity, dropping slightly on the ''ay'' and a little more on the ''ah,'' retaining the sensation of the ''ng'' point.

SNUFF ZOH ZAH EXERCISES

Purpose

These exercises open the nasal cavity and cause the singer to feel support of the lower abdominal area. They will help to even out a vibrato in the tone.

Figure 51

Figure 52

Figure 53

Figure 54

Figure 55

Procedures and Discussions

One must always do the snuff gently, but with enough energy to feel the involvement of the lower abdomen. One should never snuff so hard that any muscular action is visible in the neck. The ribs should remain wide and not drop as the exercises are being sung. If the lower abdomen does not spring out on the snuff, the shoulders will come up, packing the breath up around the throat and not allowing a full-bodied tone.

Figure 51: This exercise will open up the nasal cavity and activate the lower abdomen. The lower abdomen springs out on the snuff and one feels that it is activating the breath through each "oh," "ah," or "hum."

Figure 52: This exercise is a variation of Figure 51 using a suspended breath. This is the same type of suspended breath as when one needs to pause in the text of a song but does not want to take a breath. One feels as though the breath being used in the song has momentarily stopped. The stopping of that breath must be done with the muscles of the lower abdomen and not with the throat. The "zoh" should be sung normally, letting the tone roll. Then it should be repeated, letting the tone be "heady" (i.e., feeling as though the tones are going back and up over the soft palate.)

Figure 53: This exercise is a complete nine-tone scale with no stops. It is excellent for getting a student to let the voice "roll" and for helping him control an energetic tone as well as a heady tone. The support is the same for both types of tone.

Figure 54: This exercise is a big help in getting focus into the tone. One must be sure that the inside smile is present and that the jaw swings easily, but not too far on the very first pitch, allowing it to swing more when going over the top of the third. If the tone is shrill or harsh, the back spaces are not open. The entire scale should be sung on one breath.

Figure 55: This exercise is used to feel how a crescendo goes into the bones of the face when the singer *thinks* it there. This is a wonderful exercise to develop the forte dynamic.

SH-SH-SH AND NG-NG-NG EXERCISES

Purpose

These exercises are invaluable in developing the staccato.

Shh   shh   shh   shh   shh   (etc.)

Figure 56

Ng   ng   ng   ng   ng   ng   ng

Figure 57

Procedure

The "sh" sensation starts from the "hook" muscle area (lower part of the abdomen). The abdomen is pulled in *easily* with each "sh" until one feels it can no longer pull in. It is the "sh" sound *pulling* it in—it should not be *banged*. There is a difference. The abdomen goes in slowly and steadily, not in and out.

Figure 57 is then sung slowly, allowing the jaw to swing gently on each "ng"; the pull from the abdomen comes from the same feeling as from the "sh-sh-sh" part of the exercise. On the "ng" part of the exercise, one still feels a steady pull in, up, and back in the abdominal area, never a pumping in and out. (One does feel a pulsation at the end of the sternum.) The "ng" should have the feeling of the wide snuff and the inside smile, being sure to keep the mask wide.

After the staccato "ng" is mastered, one should sing the same pitches *legato*, the pitch being started at the same time that the jaw swings down. The student should be sure to keep the mask wide. This exercise is invaluable for increasing the high range.

Discussion

When the student gets up to the beginning of the upper range, he should let the body drop in the "rag doll" position, take a wide back-rib breath, stand erect (*easily,* not with a sudden jerk of the body) and sing the arpeggio again. If there is width in the mask, a feeling of wide space in the back, and a swinging jaw (with no weight in it), one finds that the pitches will go higher and easier, feeling no effort in the throat. The whole body is involved as it should be in all exercises.

So often, young students are started with singing staccato exercises. They begin to "pump" the abdominal muscles (which I feel is the wrong muscular action for the abdominal area). The inside spaces of the oral cavity, the soft palate particularly, are not ready to accommodate that tone. I feel it is wrong to begin on staccato work until the breath, the oral cavity, and jaw and tongue action are correct. *Then* the staccato simply "happens."

NEE-OH EXERCISE

Purpose

This exercise is used to get focus into the "oh."

Nee - oh - ee - - oh - - - ee - - oh - ee - - oh - - - ee - - oh - - ee - oh - - - ee

Figure 58

Procedure

The "n" brings the tone forward, and it is felt in the nasal septum. The sensation should be allowed to stay there. The jaw is dropped easily (not too far), and the lips are rounded *slightly* on the "oh."

Discussion

The lack of focus in an "oh" is what causes the pitch to go under. The feeling of the "nee" brought into the "oh" will give the "oh" the necessary focus to stay on pitch. One should be sure he does not lose the sensation of the tones literally being fastened into the septum when going into the "oh." When reaching the upper range of the voice, the tones should seem to go straight up through the top of the head. One feels muscular sensation in the mask on "oh," "oo" and "aw," but the mask does not feel as wide as it does on all the other vowels.

NEE-OH-(AY)-(AH)-(EYE) EXERCISE

Purpose

It will remove shrillness (whiteness) from "ay," "ah," and "eye."

Figure 59

Procedure

This exercise is sung headily through the octave jump and the vowel changes. When singing the "ay," "ah," and "eye," the mask becomes involved (it will be slightly lifted), and the space which has been felt on the "oh" is kept behind the new vowel.

FIVE-PART EXERCISE

Purpose

It will aid the singer to increase his high range.

Discussion

Each of the five parts of this exercise involve various principles related to fine singing. All of these basic principles are capitalized upon in this exercise because each step builds towards, and is included in, the final production of the arpeggio (Figure 66a). Every step promotes a better understanding of the *strong mask,* the *dome-shaped feeling* inside the mouth, the *strength* of the *soft palate,* the sensation of *strength* across the *bridge* of the *nose,* the correct use of the *upper lip,* the *jaw* and the *tongue.*

All of these principles allow the arpeggio to be correctly vocalized, with no differentiation between ranges. The five separate sections of this exercise are always sung together and in the order given.

PART 1: NING-EE AND NING-AH

Ning ee ning ee ning
Ning ah ning ah ning

Figure 60

Procedure

The upper lip should be rolled up (Figure 61), but the muscles on the bridge of the nose should not be allowed to become involved. The "ning-ee" should be sung four or five times, each a half step higher than the one before. Then there should be four or five "ning-ahs."

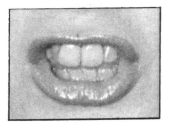

Figure 61
Rolled upper lip position for
part one of five-part exercise

Discussion

This exercise helps to bring the tone into the nasopharyngeal area and keep the tone focused. One feels a warmth in the upper lip after doing this exercise. This involvement of the upper lip should be carried over into the next exercise.

PART 2: HEADY NEE AND NEE-AH

Procedure

This section of the exercise is sung very lightly. The upper lip is in a normal position, but there is a feeling of strength in the lip that comes from the

Figure 62

preceding part of the exercise. The "heady" tones feel as though they are riding on a wave of air over the soft and hard palate.

The heady "nee" is sung entirely in the middle range with each repetition ascending in half steps. The jaw should not drop but rather remain loose at the hinge as the figure ascends and descends. The only variation in the heady "nee-ah" is that the "ah" is sung on the descending tone sequence, dropping the jaw very very slightly, from the hinge. *The jaw should remain loose, however.*

Discussion

This section of the five-part exercise gently aids the feeling of opening the back spaces and causes the inside pull-ups to come into play through production of the "ee" and "ah." Because the "ee" is very bright, the mask should feel strong, with a great width under the eyes and a dome-shaped feeling inside the mouth. The wide-opened spaces inside the mouth are especially needed as the figure ascends.

The jaw does not move on the heady "ah" as much as it would on a "mixed" tone, so that the inside pull-ups (arch) can become involved, causing them to be strengthened.

PARTS 3 AND 4: THEE-THAH AND THAH-THEE

Procedure

These exercises are used to eliminate pressure on the tongue, helping the tongue to be wide and loose as well as to coordinate the action of the tongue

Figure 63

Thah—— thee—— thah—— thee—— thah

Figure 64

and jaw. The mask must be strong and wide, the cushions lifted under the eyes, and there must be a sensation of extreme strength across the bridge of the nose as well as of the inside smile. The tongue is resting gently on the lower lip (Figure 65). The figures are sung lightly and the singer must be sure to arch over* on the top pitch of the triplet. The muscles in the back of the tongue should never feel pulled. The "th" must be unvoiced (as in "think," *not* as in "this").

One finds that, as a result of these exercises, great strength is created under the eyes as the cushions remain lifted throughout and more space is

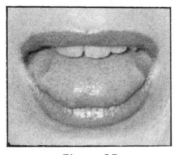

Figure 65
Tongue position for parts three and four
of five-part exercise

created around the soft palate area. The jaw swings straight down like that of a puppet, the cushions remaining lifted.

Both exercises should be practiced no more than three or four times (or less, initially) since the muscles of the tongue are in an abnormal position and will tire very easily.

Discussion

There are some potential problems with the tongue which must be corrected in order to perform these exercises properly. It is almost impossible to sing these exercises correctly if the tongue is "grooved" or "pressed." The exercises should be tried, but always do this gently, never forcing the tongue or

---

*"Arch over" means for the singer to be sure to feel that he is singing on the "top" of each note by feeling the tone go up and over the soft and hard palate.

pulling it out. Corrective exercises for the tongue (Chapter 9) should be used in conjunction with this. These exercises *must* be sung forward.

PART 5: NEE-AH-EE-AH-EE-AH-EE EXERCISE

Nee- -ah - -ee - - ah- - ee- - ah - - - ee

Figure 66a

Procedure

The entire figure is sung starting in the low range and going upward in half steps, each figure sung in one breath. The exercise is sung legato, in a normal voice, not forte or piano, using a mixed tone. The figure should be sung as high as it can be with complete ease. The jaw swings on each vowel sound (swing up on ''ee'' and down on 'ah'') and on the initial ''n,'' making sure that the first and last tones of the arpeggio are sung lightly.

After getting to the top range, bring the exercise back down, skipping a third each time.

Discussion

The principles basic to the previous four parts are coordinated in singing the final arpeggio:

(a) The inside smile activates the soft palate, the inside pull-ups giving a dome-like feeling inside the mouth; the corners of the mouth are turned slightly upward (smiling *easily,* not grimacing).

(b) Because of the inside smile there is a strong mask, with the cushions lifted; a great muscular width and strength is felt under the eyes, presenting a sensation of a squareness of the facial area, from which the jaw can swing down easily.

(c) The jaw and tongue move together as one unit; the tongue is resting front and wide.

(d) One feels strength over the bridge of the nose throughout the exercise, the first tone starting headily focused through the nasopharyngeal area (but *not* to the extreme).

(e) The upper lip is in a normal position, but one feels strength which helps the action of the inside pull-ups and the muscles over the bridge of the nose; the involved (*inside*) pull-up of the upper lip will keep the vowels focused.

One must concentrate on the important action of the jaw. Many times the jaw will stick on the second "ee" because the jaw is not swinging, but is remaining stationary or "set." It is very important to keep the jaw loose, moving it *slightly* on each of the vowel sounds (from the width under the eyes, keeping the mask strong and the back opened).

When one reaches the beginning of the upper range, the inside smile is very much involved. In this upper range, the top note will start "shooting" straight up to the top of the head. The width of the mask goes all the way into the temples. The jaw should swing further on the higher tones.

Since the arpeggio is sung rather quickly, the jaw must essentially swing its way through, springing lightly; the tongue should not be pressing, grooving or bunching. When swinging the jaw in the upper range, a strength should be felt over the bridge of the nose and the upper lip should feel strong and wide so that there will be focus.

When the tone is not spinning easily as the singer is ascending, he should stop and do the complete wide snuff between arpeggios. He should then sing the exercise, finding that the top pitch "pops" over into the head very easily. He can also drop over and do the rag doll and, while dropped over, do the complete wide snuff, then do half of it, rising easily, and the exercise will be performed even better.

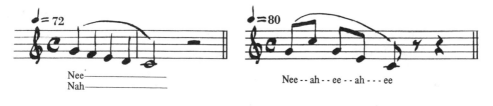

Figure 66b, part 1   **Figure 66b, part 2**

Discussion

In the high range, when the top tone of the arpeggio is not easily sung, one should stop and roll the tongue over (the tip of the tongue is behind the front teeth, the back of the tongue is arched and wide) and sing "nee" in that range as in Figure 66b, part 1. (One will feel much space in the back of the pharyngeal area.) Then "nee-ah-ee-ah-ee" should be sung as in Figure 66b, part 2, on the same notes as the corresponding notes of the arpeggio. Finally, the complete arpeggio is sung once again, keeping the same sensations in the mask, the oral cavity and the pharyngeal area. It will be found that this will assist in singing the top of the scale more easily and in an excellent vocal line.

MING MEE EXERCISES

Purpose

These exercises aid in focusing of tone. They are also excellent for getting the upper lip and the mask to work.

Figure 67a

Figure 67b

Procedure

The ''ming'' portion of Figure 67a is sung detached with the mask lifted on each ''m.'' The jaw moves gently but swings further when the exercise is sung in the higher range.

The ''mee-mah'' portion of this exercise is sung in the same way with a slight jaw action and the mask lifting on each ''m.'' During the entire exercise, the tongue remains forward, wide and soft behind the lower teeth.

Figure 67b—''Mee'': The same principles are applied for this as for the above exercise.

Discussion

The ''m'' is a good consonant to apply (like ''p'') to exercises in which the lifting of the lip and its coordination are to be developed. It starts the tone moving. Every time the ''m'' is sung, the upper lip and mask should immediately be lifted upward. The most important factor which comes into play on the "ming" is the mask. There should be a strong width under the eyes, the cushions lifted, and an inside smile.

When done correctly, the upper lip will feel a strengthening sensation. The tone will be forward and will be sensed as being focused in the nasal cavity with a buzzing across the bridge of the nose. The tone will feel as though it is bouncing off the hard palate after passing over the arch of the soft palate created by the strong mask and inside smile. Each of the tones sung should have support under them, and the abdomen should have the normal action of a controlled inward progression of the lower abdominal area.

LAH BAY DAH MAY NEE POH TOO

Purpose

This exercise uses syllables with a combination of vowels and consonants that was developed by early Italian pedagogs. It provides an excellent bridge between the vocalises and song texts. Each successive singing of the vocalise should be sung a half step higher than the preceding one.

Figure 68

MEE-OH EXERCISE

Purpose

It will develop the feeling of resonance in the nasal cavity so important in nasty tones or the "belting" tone (See Chapter 11). It will also aid in developing the back spaces.

Figure 69

Procedure

This exercise is begun in the middle range and is sung legato. The exercise is performed by first holding the nose with the thumb and index finger, pinching it off so that no air is allowed to pass in or out of it. The inside smile should *not* be activated as it is first sung.

It is then sung again, the inside smile is added, and the tone is not nasal. These pairs (one nasal, one with back spaces open) should be sung three to five times, each time ascending in half steps.

NEE-AH EXERCISE (1)

Purpose

It will develop a forte dynamic in the upper range.

Figure 70

Procedure

One should be careful not to drop the jaw too far too soon on this exercise; otherwise, the jaw will have no place to go when it needs to spring for the top note. The jaw should be checked to be sure that it is loose.

The bottom pitch should be sung very headily and should be felt as high in position as is the top pitch. The crescendo should feel as though it is going into the bones of the face, and the decrescendo should feel as though, before descending, it goes back and up over the soft palate. One should be sure that the tone stays forward on the descending part of the exercise.

NEE-AH EXERCISE (2)

Purpose

It will enable the upper pitches to "spin" high in the head.

Figure 71

Procedure

The singer should adhere to the instructions outlined for Figure 70 regarding the feeling in the jaw and how to sing the bottom tone. The tone should feel as though the top goes straight through the top of the head, *not the mask*.

NEE-AH EXERCISE (3)

Purpose

It is used to develop the upper range.

Figure 72

Procedure

The "nee" must be sung very headily and in a high position from the first pitch onward. The descending passage likewise must be sung headily, arching over each note to the next.

The jaw must not swing too far too soon, and the singer must be sure to let it swing *easily* on the top pitch.

8

EXERCISES AND TECHNIQUES
FOR CORRECTING VOCAL PROBLEMS

During the study of the basic and advanced exercises and during the singing of vocal literature, vocal problems will be noted which make singing difficult—vocal problems such as grooved, pressed, bunched and pulled-up tip of tongue; shaking, jutting and stiff jaw; nasality; wobble; sharping; flatting; etc. These problems are caused by incorrect coordination of the physiological and anatomical systems.

It is of great importance that the student, as well as the teacher of voice, be aware of the possible physical damage certain vocal techniques might cause in singing. Any manipulation of the tongue or the larynx, or the holding of the jaw, is a wrong approach to singing. Likewise, a technique which calls for the tongue to be pressed is also incorrect. Since some of the muscles of the tongue attach to the hyoid bone (see Figure 6c), pressing or grooving the tongue obviously must restrict the movement of the larynx to a certain degree. (The larynx is simply suspended in the throat and should have no feeling of restriction in any way.) Some of the muscles from the tongue also are connected to the soft palate; therefore, any pressing down of the tongue would pull down the soft palate. This is just the opposite of what we wish.

The vocal mechanism should be free of any pathological abnormalities. If a teacher has any idea that something is physically wrong with a student's vocal mechanism, he should send him immediately to a laryngologist. A teacher should never work "in the dark," wondering why the vocal sound is not all that it should be.

Emotional problems also have a great influence on the voice. While I was studying in New York there was a certain period when my voice was not functioning as it had been, even though I was at this time working with Maude Douglas Tweedy. I went to see one of the city's top laryngologists. He looked at my throat and said that the cords were perfect in every way. He then asked me if I was under any emotional strain and I said that I was. He explained to me that when a singer is under emotional stress, the cords tend to stiffen and therefore do not function as easily as they do under normal conditions.

For the duration of this period of stress my vocalizing was kept lighter than usual, and I never made maximum demands of my voice. As soon as I was relieved of the emotional strain, the voice returned to its previous freedom.

A number of times students of mine have been well prepared vocally for a senior or master recital, and just prior to that recital have experienced a devastating emotional situation. Immediately, their voices were affected. However, in life, "the show must go on," and we must not completely give in to our emotional upsets or, on the other hand, make excessive demands on the voice.

The voice is also affected by psychological problems. Many times a singer can be greatly helped by seeking professional counseling from an excellent psychiatrist or psychologist. The professional will be able to uncover problems in that student's life which are beyond the realm of the vocal teacher.

The beginning stages of voice study should not emphasize the vocal problems at all but should involve the basic study of the production of sound and the correct method of breathing. The tongue problem (as well as any other vocal problem) will be present at the onset of study if it is there at all; but only after the breath and basic body coordination have been somewhat mastered should the singer attempt to correct vocal problems. Correcting poor vocal coordination should be pursued at a moderate pace by beginning corrective exercises *one at a time*. If great emphasis is placed on the "vocal inabilities," then a reverse process of learning can easily take over. Since correcting goes slowly, the emphasis on vocal problems should be slight and given only over a long period of time.

The exercises and techniques described below are based on Dr. F.E. Miller's years of experience with laryngeal problems. They are designed to correct improper modifications of the voice and physical problems, as well as to help alleviate the effects, and many times the causes, of certain pathological findings. If these exercises are practiced correctly with great concentration, vocal problems such as those described before can be corrected and good basic technique will ultimately be developed.

NASALITY

Since a singer's goal is to communicate a vocal text in a beautiful way, it is necessary that the quality of the voice projecting the song be warm and that the tones resonate fully. Nasality affects the projection of the text, its meaning and color, and does not allow good resonance to take place. The singer who sings with a nasal tone, therefore, should work with corrective exercises to eliminate this unwanted tone quality. If the problem is acute and seems to hinder the student's progress, he should see a laryngologist to determine whether there is a medical basis for the nasal tone. It is important for the teacher and the student to know exactly what problems they are dealing with and just how they should be working in order to overcome them.

The nasal tone in singing, as well as in speech, is caused by the tone resonating completely in the nasopharyngeal cavities, with no feeling of the soft palate being activated. Because the tone is based in the nose, the resulting unpleasant sound is one that is biting and shrill. There are, of course, certain colors which are employed in singing which require nasal tone (e.g., nastiness, spite, etc.), but these are used for certain coloring and phrasing effects and should not be considered part of the "finished" tone (See Chapter 11).

Many forms of "functional" nasality in the singing voice are caused by the inability of the soft palate to move. An easy way to see the difference between a relaxed soft palate and an active soft palate (Figures 73 and 74) can be easily illustrated by looking at the uvula by using a hand mirror.

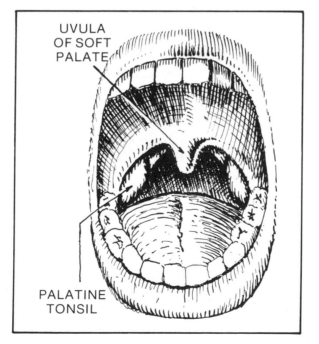

Figure 73
Soft palate (relaxed)

The position of the uvula varies with the individual, but it can be impossible to see when there is a lazy soft palate. Sometimes it lies on the back of the tongue. It can also be completely covered by the bunching of the tongue in the back. The soft palate remains inactive in those positions. If the soft palate is

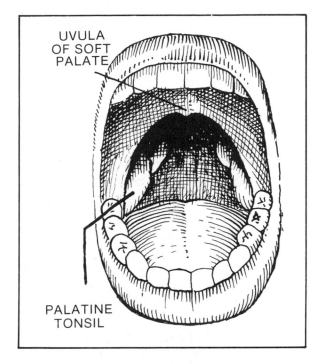

Figure 74
Soft palate (active)

kept in this position, any tone passing from the larynx to the pharyngeal resonating cavities is directed upward toward the nasopharyngeal area and is allowed to resonate there independent of the other resonating cavities (such as the mouth and the throat). The resultant sound is nasal.

If the nasality can be traced to an inactive soft palate, the following exercises can be employed to strengthen the muscles connecting the soft palate to the tongue and the hard palate. Since the muscles involved in moving the soft palate are small, it is important that these exercises be practiced only a few times a day. The development of strength in this area will come over a period of time and should be slow and careful.

AH-AH-AH EXERCISE

Purpose

This exercise is used to strengthen the soft palate.

Procedure

While looking at the back of the mouth with the mirror, an "ah" should be headily spoken three or four times on one breath, employing a portamento downward, then back up, on the "ah." This exercise should be done very lightly and at a higher pitch level than normal speech. The beginning of the "ah" should use a strong wide mask with the cushions raised. The jaw should remain loose and open throughout the exercise and should not be allowed to come back up when descending. The sensation is that of an audible sigh.

Discussion

As can be readily seen in the mirror, the soft palate arches upward when the "ah" is made. This arched position allows the best resonance for each tone. Practicing this exercise three and four times a day will help give the soft palate the flexibility it needs for resonance and for eventual performance of coloratura literature. A strong soft palate is also the basis for an even vibrato or shimmer in the voice. Since all "k" exercises (Chapters 6 and 7) activate the soft palate, they are imperative in eliminating nasality.

An inactive soft palate may be caused by different things. One cause can be organic pathology such as scar tissue surrounding the pillars (which are perpendicular to the back of the tongue and rising upward to the soft palate). Surgical removal of the tonsils can cause scar tissue to form in this manner. Using corrective exercises over a period of time will strengthen the muscles which control the movement of the soft palate. Usually, a "lazy" soft palate is caused by the singer's not having previously learned the proper way to exercise the fine muscles which activate the soft palate.

ROLLED TONGUE EXERCISE

Purpose

It will widen and loosen the tongue and strengthen the soft palate.

Figure 75

Procedure

This exercise should not be practiced more than three times on each vowel and should be done very lightly. It should be practiced with a mirror since the position of the tongue is so important (Figure 76). The tongue is rolled forward *slightly* with the tip of the tongue touching the back of the lower teeth. The upper back teeth will touch the back part of the tongue slightly (especially when vocalizing the ''ee'').

When the correct position is learned and is easily coordinated, the exercise is continued by vocalizing the tone sequence on ''nee'' in one breath in the middle range, arching between each note; the exercise should be sung in head voice very gently. The sequence should then be repeated on the vowel sound ''nah'' in the same manner as ''nee'' was sung. Because this exercise involves a great deal of muscular action, it should be practiced no more than three times on each vowel, each time a half step higher than the preceding scale. After the mask and the cushions are in position, the jaw should swing on the first note and remain loose throughout the scale; it should *not* move on each of the five tones.

Discussion

If the tongue ''bunches'' (i.e., pulls up too high, touching the hard palate), the tone will be nasal and constricted, since it is resonating only in the nasopharyngeal area. It is best, then, to gently roll the tongue forward a few times in the ''rolled tongue'' position and then bring it back to its resting state. This action should not be forced and should be free of muscular strain.

Often, the tongue will shake as this exercise is performed. If such is the case, the exercise should be practiced not more than one or two times on each vowel sound until the tongue is loosened and can more readily be rolled over.

The position and action of the mask and jaw are extremely important to this exercise. The mask should remain wide and strong with the cushions lifted throughout the exercise. This mask involvement allows the arch inside the mouth to maintain that position which allows the best production of the bright sounds "ee" and "ah". This arch brings the vowel sounds forward over the soft palate, keeping them from falling back into the throat.

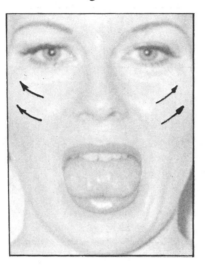

Figure 76
Tongue and mask positions for
rolled tongue exercise

THE IRREGULAR VIBRATO

There are many vibratos which are unpleasant to listen to (i.e., too fast, too slow, or uneven) and which can be modified to be more effective in expressing the vocal text and line.

Poor breath support and soft palate strength are main factors which affect the vibrato and cause it to become an objectionable "tremolo." They act upon the tone production so as to make the vibrato too slow, fast, or take on an uneven waver. It is therefore necessary that a singer have complete control of the exhalation of his air. Tone production must be supported by an even flow of controlled air. The abdominal muscles must be strong and properly coordinated so that the process of breathing while singing supports the tone and gives it a beautiful warm shimmer.

Inactivity of the soft palate is another cause of the tremolo. The exercises given below can be used to overcome the wide, fast, irregular vibrato.

TABLE A

EXERCISES TO CORRECT
THE IRREGULAR VIBRATO

Exercise	Appropriate Chapter
Strengthen the soft palate	
Wide Snuff (Figure 47)	7
Snuff Zoh–Snuff Zah (Figures 51, 52, 53)	7
"K" exercises	
Kee kay (Figure 24)	6
Kah-kay-kee-koh-koo (Figure 41)	7
Kee-kah-kee (Figure 42)	7
Strengthen breath support and control	
Hum-Portamento (Figures 78a, 78b)	8
Hee-ah (Figure 23)	6
Waw-ee (Figure 49)	7
Circle-arm breath (Figures 35, 36, 37, 38)	7
Waw-ee-ah	8
Rag doll	7
Hum-mee (Figure 77)	8

HUM-MEE AND HUM-MAH EXERCISE

Purpose

This exercise develops the breath support as well as the soft palate.

Figure 77

Procedure

In this exercise, one feels terrific air pressure against the hard and soft palate and the cushions under the eyes. The back ribs work very hard as do the lower abdominal muscles.

WAW-EE-AH EXERCISE

Procedure

The "waw" exercise (Figure 49) can be modified, taking the "ee" to 6 and changing to "ah," then descending from 6 to 1. It is important to move rapidly to 6 to insure strong support at the top of this exercise.

HUM-PORTAMENTO EXERCISES

Figure 78a   Figure 78b

Procedure

The same sensations apply as those felt on the "hum-mee" and "hum-mah" exercises (Figure 77).

TONGUE PROBLEMS

The tongue directly affects the sound of a tone. It is easy to see why it is so important that the action of the tongue be complementary to the act of singing. "The tongue is so poised, adjusted and balanced that it is capable of an endless variety of complicated movements."[1] The tongue must therefore maintain the position that will allow it to act only to make possible correct tone production, phonation, and articulation.

The most correct position of the tongue is when it lies wide and soft against the lower teeth (Figure 79), moving freely with the jaw every time the tongue changes position for different vowels. The "ah" has a level tongue; on

---

[1]Dr. Frank E. Miller, *Vocal Art Science,* (New York, G. Schirmer, Inc., 1922)

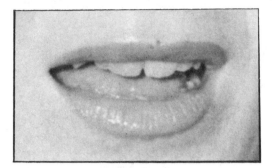

Figure 79
Correct position of tip of tongue

"ay" the tongue arches, the sides touching the molar teeth; on "eye" the tongue is wide until the second half of the diphthong "ee" causes it to lift slightly; on "ih", "a" and "eh" the tongue is wide, but arched; on "uh" the tongue is level; and on "oh" and "oo" the tongue is very slightly dropped in the center but never pressed or leaving the back of the lower front teeth. The tip of the tongue should *not* be allowed to pull upward behind the upper teeth (as shown in Figure 80); this position constricts the tone and changes the vowel sound. The normal position of the tongue is modified for the rolled "r" which involves the tip.

TABLE B

EXERCISES USED TO CORRECT TONGUE IRREGULARITIES

Exercise	Appropriate Chapter
Gah	8
Ng-ah	8
Thee-thah** (Figure 63)	7
Thah-thee** (Figures 64, 65)	7
Nee (Figure 75)	8
Nah (Figure 75)	8

**This exercise is described in Chapter 7 under the *Five-part exercise*.

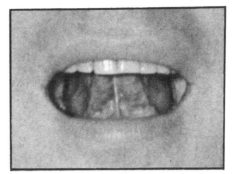

Figure 80
Pulled up tongue (incorrect)

There are many irregular positions and actions of the tongue. If the tongue "bunches," "presses," "grooves," or "pulls" during singing, all of the related anatomy (i.e., soft palate, pharynx, etc.) will be pulled out of their correct alignments as well.

The *pressed* tongue (Figure 81) comes from extreme muscular action of the tongue, causing it to pull downward into the jaw; the tone produced this way is almost always guttural.

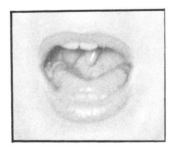

Figure 81
Pressed tongue (incorrect)

The *grooved* tongue (Figure 82) also is caused by extreme muscular action, pulling the tongue down into the jaw but also forming a groove on the surface of the tongue.

The *bunched* tongue is caused by muscular action which pushes the tongue upward, bending it so that the center of the tongue practically touches or rests against the hard palate and soft palate. This position blocks the air flow through the mouth and changes the shape of the oral resonating cavity. The bunched tongue and its effect on the tone is similar to the effect that stuffing cloth into the end of a clarinet would have on the sound coming from that instrument.

One other tongue position which is considered irregular is the *pulled*

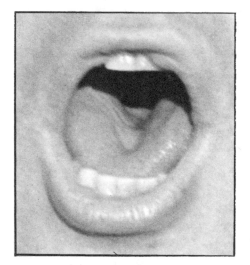

Figure 82
Grooved tongue (incorrect)

position (Figure 83); i.e., when the tip of the tongue is pulled upward towards the upper teeth and slightly back. This position also changes the sound. *The tongue should never be pulled back.*

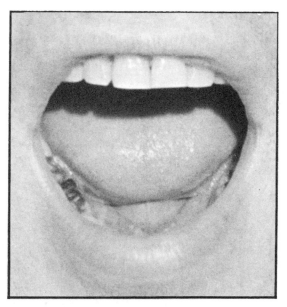

Figure 83
Pulled back tongue (incorrect)

The following two exercises will seem to be a contradiction of what has been expressed consistently in this book: *the jaw and tongue should always move together*. These exercises are designed to eliminate specific tongue problems. Even though they call for a certain independence of the jaw and tongue for a specific purpose, it should be noted that the jaw and tongue *do* move together on the *final* part of each exercise.

NG-AH EXERCISE

Purpose

It will correct the pressed or pulled tongue.

Procedure

To be effective, this exercise should be practiced daily. There should be width under the eyes and the jaw should be dropped, leaving it dropped as the tongue is lifted from the back, keeping the tip against the lower front teeth. As the back of the tongue is gently lifted up, the sound "ng" should be spoken with the jaw remaining still; the tongue falls back as the syllable "ah" is spoken. This should be done four times, loosening the back tongue muscles. On the fifth spoken "ng-ah" the jaw should come up and be allowed to swing down as the fifth "ng-ah" is spoken. After this exercise has been practiced by speaking the syllables, it should be further practiced by singing the exercise on one pitch.

GAH EXERCISE

Purpose

This exercise is especially effective for correcting the badly pressed tongue.

Procedure

It is performed like the previous exercise, but without the "ng" sound preceeding the "gah." The mask is lifted, the jaw is dropped, and the back of the tongue is lifted to sound "gah." The exercise should be practiced by first speaking, then singing the "gah" five times on one pitch. This exercise reaches further back than the "ng-ah." The "g" is extremely effective in lifting the back of the tongue, but it should be vocalized very lightly on each tone.

Enunciating the syllable "gah" should involve the mask. The cushions should be raised with a feeling of strength under the eyes and over the bridge of the nose. The soft palate will then automatically lift, allowing the tongue and jaw to move freely.

****

All exercises which I use to correct tongue irregularities have been described in this book and are indicated in Table B. These exercises should be practiced with great concentration. One should always remember that correcting tongue problems is a slow process. Trying to get the tongue to go into a certain position is a constant battle. As each exercise is practiced over a period of time, the involuntary nervous system eventually will take over the control of the tongue muscles and the tongue will act in a correct way without the singer's having to constantly be aware of its position.

INCORRECT LIP FORMATION

The correct musculature of the inside smile can produce very different visible results in different singers (Figures 84a, 84b, 84c). If one has a short upper lip it should not be pulled sharply down to cover the teeth. When the lip is pulled down over the teeth, it causes the tone to become nasal and the tones are never well articulated.

Some basic structural problems tend to cause the singer to consciously pull the lip down; unattractive teeth can do this. As shown in Figure 85, the short upper lip allows the teeth to show, so a singer with this kind of lip may,

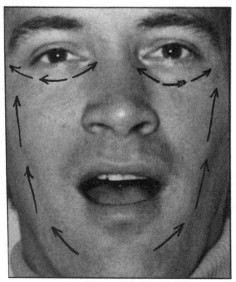

Figure 84a
Facial position while using inside smile (male)

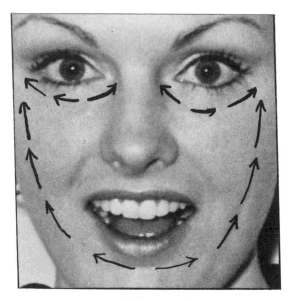

Figure 84b
Facial position while using inside smile (female)

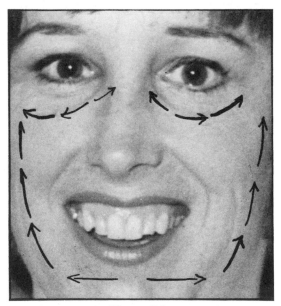

Figure 84c
Facial position while using inside smile (female)

over a period of years, have built up a habit of pulling the lip down over the upper teeth in order to hide them. Doing this greatly hinders good tone production and good enunciation.

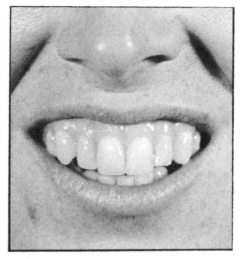

Figure 85
Short upper lip

If the singer has a short upper lip and if he is used to pulling his lip down constantly in order to hide the teeth, he should use the "preh" exercises (Figure 33). The "p" should pull the upper lip upwards; the "preh's" should be practiced daily to get the upper lip to be in its correct position. Another exercise is the "ning-ee, ning-ah," the first part of the five-part exercise (Figure 60).

VOCAL PROBLEMS ORIGINATING WITH THE JAW

The jaw's placement and movement are very important in affecting resonance, phonation and the vocal line. The muscles of the larynx and the tongue, as well as the muscles which hold the jaw to the skull, are directly related to the jaw. Depending upon its alignment and its movement, the jaw can easily change the formation and production of words as well as alter the resonance of each tone.

For the best tone production and resonance, as well as the best enunciation of words, the jaw should remain relaxed and loose. As the jaw swings—and it is important to realize that the movement of the jaw should be a swinging action, not dropped or forced—the tongue should follow the jaw down and up. Because all of the anatomy intrinsic to singing (pharynx, neck, head and tongue muscles, etc.) are so distinctly interrelated, the jaw should always swing from the wide mask position and straight down from the hinge (Figure 86a).

The jaw should *never* be stiff as it moves or rests; it should *not* jut outward (Figure 86b) or move to either side (Figure 87), and it should not shake. All

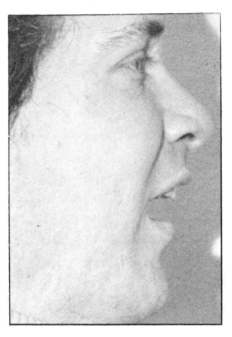

Figure 86a
Correct swing of the jaw

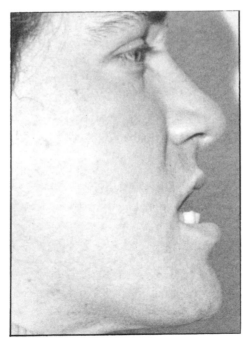

Figure 86b
Jaw jutting forward (incorrect)

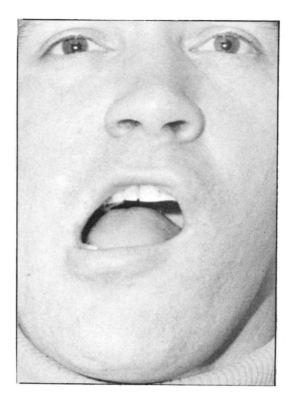

Figure 87
Jaw moving to the side (incorrect)

these incorrect movements and positions of the jaw can affect a good tone production and resonance, phonation, and vocal line.

THE SHAKING JAW

There are many reasons why the jaw might shake while a person is singing. Tension in the muscles of the jaw itself or an incorrect jaw position can cause the jaw to shake; a locked flow of breath is another major cause. It is important to work with the exercises which strengthen the appropriate muscles so that they will function better and allow the jaw to swing freely and loosely.

The muscles of the tongue and soft palate (''inside pull-ups'') should be worked intensely to eventually allow the jaw to feel freer. One should emphasize exercises which strengthen the soft palate, relax the tongue, and improve the flow of air. The rolled tongue exercises (Figures 75 and 76) as described in this chapter under ''tongue irregularities'' should be given when beginning to work with the jaw problem and should be used in conjunction with the following exercises.

SIT-UP EXERCISE

Purpose

It will coordinate breathing with vocalizing.

Figure 88

Procedure

This exercise is vocalized while doing a "sit-up" exercise. The back and legs lie flat on the floor with the feet tucked under a chair (if needed to keep the heels on the floor). The torso comes to a sitting-up position on the portamento on "hee"; the octave is sung on "ah," the back is straight, the tail bone tucked under, with the head in a level position. The body remains in the sitting-up position as the remainder of the sequence (5, 3, 1) is sung on the "ah."

Discussion

Often when this exercise is sung, the jaw will unexpectedly perform correctly (without shaking). The flow of the breath will be unlocked with this exercise.

When working with this exercise, all of the principles basic to singing bright vowels (i.e., strong mask, cushions lifted, etc.) should be employed. The jaw should swing on the initiation of the "ah" and the tongue should follow it, lying wide and soft against the lower teeth.

THE STIFF JAW

The movement of the stiff jaw is severely restricted and therefore does not allow the voice to have good resonance, tone initiation, phonation or articulation. Words cannot be spoken, let alone sung, correctly without involvement of the jaw. Generally, if the jaw is held stiffly with muscular pressure, the tones produced and the words articulated will form in the back of the throat creating muffled, guttural sounds. They are unpleasant to listen to as well as being relatively inaudible.

The stiff jaw can be corrected with the following exercises. The movement of the jaw on each exercise is critical and should originate from the width created under the eyes. The jaw should swing very loosely, like that of a puppet, from the temples straight down from the strength and width created through the mask.

FAH-EE-AH-EE AND FEE-AH-EE-AH EXERCISES

Purpose

They will train the jaw to swing freely.

Figure 89

Procedure

These exercises are vocalized in one breath in the middle range; the entire sequence is sung legato. Each exercise should be practiced four to five times, each time ascending in half steps. After going up, each exercise should then be sung two to three times down the scale.

Discussion

On the first set of syllables, the jaw should swing on the "fah" and should come back up on the "ee." The jaw simply swings loosely from the width created under the eyes. The "f" is initiated by lightly laying the upper teeth on the lower lip; the lips should be soft and responsive (not tight and spread). The air is simply passed through the upper teeth across the soft lower lip as the "f" is aspirated on the first tone of the sequence. These same principles apply to the second set of syllables.

HUM-MAH AND HUM-MAY EXERCISES

Purpose

They will train the jaw to swing freely, coordinating the swing with the inside smile.

Figure 90

Procedure

These exercises are sung in one breath in the middle range, with one tone arching over to the next. The jaw action should be exactly as described in the preceding exercise, swinging loosely from the strength under the eyes all the way into the temples, the jaw swinging on each "h" of the "hum." The tongue follows it, lying wide and soft against the bottom teeth.

Discussion

The "h" is aspirated very lightly on each of the tones of the sequence by releasing air through the mouth as a result of pressure of the abdominal muscles. Each tone is connected so the attack of the "h" should be done very lightly.

KAH-KEE-KOH EXERCISE

Purpose

It will train the jaw to swing freely.

Figure 91

Procedure

This exercise is sung in the middle range, each time ascending a half step. It is sung very lightly and never too slowly. The inside smile must be present.

Discussion

Each tone is arched over to the following tone, the "k" aspirated each time with the abdominal muscles. The mask should be maintained throughout the "kah" and "kee" part of the exercise, the width created under the eyes and the cushions activated. There is no mask in "koh," but the tone simply goes straight up through the hard palate. The jaw swings on each of the "k's."

THE JUTTING JAW

The jutting jaw protrudes straight forward from the face. This position hampers phonation, articulation, and resonance of tone (Figure 86b).

The "flah-flah-nee" exercise (Figure 25) is useful as a corrective exercise to eliminate this problem. It should be used in conjunction with the exercises described above for the stiff jaw.

It is important to practice these exercises while using two mirrors. Doing this enables one to see a profile of the jaw and will allow a complete view of the jaw as it moves and positions itself during the act of singing. If the jaw goes off-center even slightly, that movement changes the air column of the oral cavity, and therefore the tone quality.

VOCAL NODES

A vocal node is nothing more than an accumulation of fibrous tissue on the vocal cords, somewhat like a corn which forms on the toe; in both cases, the accumulation of tissue is caused by increased rubbing or friction against opposing surfaces (Figure 92).

A node can be detected while singing. Often, a singer may have trouble maintaining a certain pitch, or there may be breaks in the tone which are not seemingly caused by lack of breath support. Usually, these pitch problems are caused by nodes. A vocal node can also cause a speaking voice to be extremely husky and reedy.

An easy measuring device for locating the presence of a node is the "oo"; it often will not phonate if a vocal node is present. If one suspects a node is present, it is extremely important that a throat specialist be consulted immediately to determine the degree of seriousness.

Nodes are generally caused by: (1) lack of breath support; (2) indiscriminate use of the singing voice (oversinging, improper technique used for special vocal colors, screaming, singing while tired, etc.); (3) speaking incorrectly; or (4) incorrect tongue action.

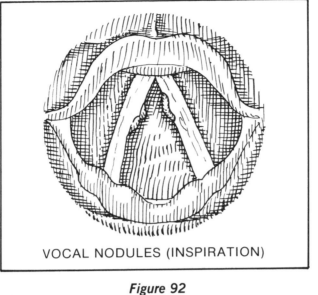

VOCAL NODULES (INSPIRATION)

Figure 92
Vocal folds with nodes

The breathing exercises described in Chapters 6 and 7 should be practiced diligently before any other corrective exercises are attempted, and one ''hook'' should precede each of the exercises given for the vocal node problem. The exercises described in this chapter under ''tongue irregularities'' should be used in conjunction with the following exercises.

HAH-HAY-HEE-HOH-HOO EXERCISE

Purpose

It will activate the lower abdominal muscles in order to develop support.

Figure 93

Procedure

This exercise is sung entirely on one tone, preferably in the middle range, and is done very easily, as marked, with a breath between each syllable. The "h" is placed on the tone with the action of the abdominal muscles.

FLAH-FLAH EXERCISE

Purpose

It will help the singer to obtain coordination between the tongue and the jaw.

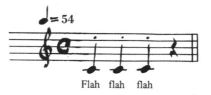

Flah   flah   flah

Figure 94

Procedure

This exercise is sung on one breath and in the middle range, each time going up a half step. The "f" is produced by allowing the air to ride through the upper teeth as they lie on the bottom lip. The tongue and jaw should move as one unit on the "fl" of each tone, the tongue lying soft and wide against the lower teeth.

Discussion

The position of the soft palate is extremely important in this exercise. The inside smile must be present, with a great strength felt across the bridge of the nose and under the eyes. The related sensation inside the mouth should be one of great space—an arch created by the high soft palate.

KEE-KAY-KEE-KAH EXERCISE

Purpose

It will help to develop the strength of the soft palate.

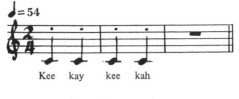

Figure 95

Procedure

The exercise is sung entirely on one tone, preferably in the middle range, and is done very lightly on one breath. The "k," most effective in activating the soft palate, is produced by action of the abdominal muscles. The "ee" and "ah" are focused, but one must keep an open feeling in the back of the mouth. The mask, therefore, should be activated and the jaw should swing loosely from the width created under the eyes.

MAH-MAH EXERCISE

Purpose

It will develop the feeling of the inside smile.

Figure 96

Procedure

The entire exercise is sung on one tone in the middle range and is done so four or five times on one breath (but not legato), always going upwards in half steps. The "m" is placed on each tone by lightly touching the lips together and then pulling the upper lip upward. There should be a feeling of great strength across the bridge of the nose as the "m" is sung.

It is very important that there be great concentration on the feeling of the inside smile in this exercise. The soft palate is easily activated by this exercise if the mask remains strong and the cushions raised.

HUM-EE AND HUM-AH EXERCISES

Purpose

It will help to develop the feeling of the inside smile.

Figure 97

Procedure

The "hum-ee" is vocalized on one tone in the middle range and should be raised one-half step each time it is sung. It should be vocalized in a flowing easy way. The jaw should swing loosely on the beginning of the "h" (coming up again for the "m") and should swing again on the bright sound "ee." The mask should be wide because of the inside smile, and strong, with the cushions under the eyes lifted.

On "hum-ah," all these same principles apply.

****

Vocal nodes cannot disappear overnight. Only through constant application of good vocal technique and through using therapeutic exercises can the nodes be gotten rid of and a healthy free voice restored. Surgical removal usually is not necessary. If the vocal node is malignant, then it is up to the laryngologist to make the decision regarding surgery.

VOCAL PROBLEMS IN GENERAL

All the exercises in this chapter involve the total coordination required for good singing; their use, therefore, is naturally corrective. Before starting any specific exercise for a problem, the basic exercises (Chapter 6) should be done. (This does not apply to nodes. This problem and its exercises should be completely set apart from any other series of exercises until the nodes are gone.)

It is important to distinguish which of a student's problems are primary ones that should be dealt with through the use of vocal exercises. Too much emphasis on vocal inabilities and vocal problems can turn the singer away with negative feelings about vocal technique per se. Exercises for specific problems should therefore be introduced with restraint and should be given over a period of time through insight into the existing vocal problems. Dr. F.E. Miller stated:

> . . . since it is impossible to bring out the subtlest points in any written set of vocalises, careful diagnosis, with careful watchfulness over the development of the pupil's voice, and slight changes to meet every new condition that arises, are essential.
>
> [The teacher] is aware that any moment the student's tone may necessitate an immediate decision on the teacher's part to change from one exercise to another, or even from one kind of exercise to another, in order to meet a new phase of development.[2]

When a student has been incapacitated by a heavy cold or has had complete vocal rest for a period of a month (and all singers should take one month out of the year for a complete rest) the following exercises should be used when the student begins vocalizing again. It should be noted that these exercises are not in the same order as they were when introducing the student to the technique. They should be done as follows:

Fah-ee-ah-ee, Fee-ah-ee-ah (Figure 89)

Hum-mah, hum-may (Figure 90)

Kee-kay-kee-kah (Figure 95)

Hum-ee, hum-ah (Figure 97)

Mah mah mah (Figure 96)

Kee-kay-kee-kah (Figure 95)

Kah-kee-koh (Figure 91)

Ning-ee, ning-ah (Figure 28)

Ng (5-4-3-2-1) (Figure 29)

Ng (5-4-3-2-1-2-3-4-5-4-3-2-1) (Figure 30)

---

[2]Ibid.

9

SINGING VOWELS AND CONSONANTS:
A COMPREHENSIVE TECHNIQUE
FOR CORRECT DICTION

Diction should never be sacrificed for tone nor should tone be sacrificed for diction. *One should always aid the other.* Learning correct diction in song is very important to the flow of the vocal line and only a comprehensive technique which teaches the molding or shaping of each vowel and consonant sound can effectively produce that flow.

EVERY VOWEL HAS ITS OWN SHAPE

The formation of correct vowels does not have to be complicated. As Dr. Frank E. Miller has stated, "The vocal mechanism is at one and the same time a sound-maker and shaper. The vocal bands, the lips of voice, initiate the song . . . leaving tongue and lips to carry out and perfect the design."[1]

When the vowel shape is correct by involving all the necessary components—lips, oral cavity, nasopharynx, oropharynx, and breath support—then and *only* then, can one get the best control of the voice.

Good diction is dependent upon the correct shape of each vowel. Each vowel has its own "home." Let us take two extremes: "ee" and "oh." We do not want the "ee" to have the same sound as the "oh," but we wish them to remain in the same vocal line. An "ee" is the most focused and front of all the vowels. "Oh" has an entirely different, less forward "home."

"Ay" is very close to the same "shape" as the "ee"; the "ah" feels as

---

[1]Frank E. Miller, *Vocal Art Science,* (New York, G. Schirmer, Inc., 1922)

143

though it is arched from one molar across the top of the mouth to the other molar tooth.

The "eye" should be pronounced as a vowel even though it is technically a diphthong. It feels as though it goes straight across the roof of the mouth and is further front than "ah."

"Oh" feels as though it goes straight up through the hard palate and the soft palate with the lips slightly rounded. (If you purse the lips tightly on "oh" or "oo" it will pull these vowels out of their "home.")

The "home" of the "aw" is far back in the mouth (the farthest back of all the vowels), being formed with a completely open throat and the soft palate feeling as though it is yawning up. The "aw" feels as though it goes back up and over the soft palate.

It is important to note that the "oh," "oo" and "aw" do not involve the mask to the degree that is found in more open vowels.

A diphthong is a sound composed of two consecutive vowels in the same syllable. What causes the diphthong to happen is the movement of the tongue and the jaw. To create the sound of "ay" the tongue is wide on the first half of the sound ("eh"), the jaw coming up and making the second half ("ee"). When singing a diphthong, the stress is always on the first vowel, the second vowel being articulated very quickly. (One should remember that the tip of the tongue is always front. The tongue arches on the "ay" and the "ee" but remains wide.) The second half of the diphthong, "ee," is caused by the jaw coming up, *jaw and tongue moving together*. I feel that words such as "new" are not diphthongs, but should be considered to be a glide between a consonant and a vowel: "n-yoo."

While "oh" is not a diphthong, it does have a slide at the end to "oo" so the same principles apply as with diphthongs.

To create the "oh," the lips are rounded slightly at the end of the sound. This method is in opposition to the Italian "o" (which is open with no diphthong), where the lips do not move while singing the "o."

VARIOUS VOWEL PROBLEMS

There are many words which combine two sounds in one syllable, such as "out," for example. These should be treated as diphthongs, the lips rounding to complete "ah-oot," just as the jaw moves up to complete the "ee" in "night." In "boy," the "oy" involves the lips going to the "ee" position at the end of the word.

An understanding of the exact formulation of sounds is important to the singer. *It is a natural formation as in speaking.* However, when one is singing, the vowel sounds are quite often sustained longer than in speaking. It is therefore vital to know their "shape" or "mold."

The short vowel sounds, such as "eh," "ih," "a," and "uh" all "sit" in the area of the nasal cavity and the hard palate (See Figure 7). The student can find this ''home'' by using the muscles of the preh exercise (Figure 33). When he practices the exercise, he pulls up the lip muscles quite dramatically; when he sings literature, he feels the acquired space on the inside (Figure 98) but should not make the face required for the exercise on the outside. With this focus, the short vowels can still be sung in the higher range by keeping the width in the mask (never widening the corners of the mouth) and dropping the jaw further in the back.

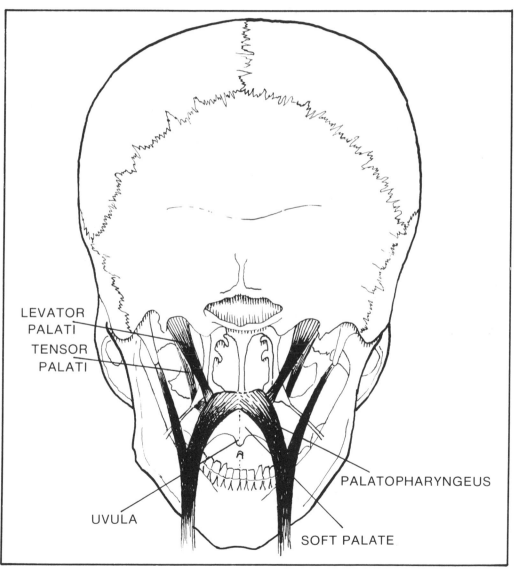

Figure 98
Muscles used while singing the "preh" exercise

The neutral vowel such as in "evil" ("il") must have a sound when it is sustained. The "il" would be sung as "ih," sustaining the vowel until the very last moment, then allowing the jaw to come up to sound a short "l."

Whenever a phrase is begun with a vowel, there should always be a feeling of an opening of the nasal area which can be accomplished by a slight inaudible snuff (which opens the nasal cavity) and by allowing the jaw to drop slightly at the hinge, with an inside smile. (This jaw swing will always prevent a glottal attack in which the vocal cords slam together and cause a harsh tone.)

Another thing which I think is very important is that when we have two words, one ending in a vowel and the next one beginning with a vowel (e.g., "the evening"), in order to avoid running them together and to articulate them well, the jaw must be allowed to drop slightly on the second word. (There should never be a glottal attack on the second vowel, the "ee" of "evening.") This principle holds whether the two vowels have the same sound or different sounds.

When one has a word ending with a consonant followed by a word begun with a vowel, e.g., "bright eyes," the "t" has a slight puff of air after it and the jaw drops slightly on the word "eyes," not "brigh teyes." Another example is "big eyes." The "g" must not be connected to the "eye" sound; this would be "bigguys." This problem is prevented once again by a puff of air and a swing of the jaw on the second word.

When there are two different consonants like "us not," there must always be a slight "air pause" between the "s" and the "n," or we have created another word, "snot." "Good aim" is another illustration of this problem; the "air pause" prevents saying the words as "good dame." It is important to remember to drop the jaw slightly on the vowel-begun "aim" to prevent a glottal attack on the "ay." "Let us pray," heard so often as "let us spray" is perhaps one of the most common errors in diction which can be solved with the "air pause" between the "s" and the "p." The "air pause" is accomplished through the snuff-zoh exercise (Figure 51).

One of the most common errors deserves special mention. It is the pronunciation of the words, "I am." If the diphthong "I" goes so far as to let the back of the tongue touch the molar teeth, the second word will be "yam." When one sings the first part of the diphthong "I" and allows the jaw to drop quickly on the "a" of "am," this will be prevented from happening. Again the "snuff-zoh" exercise (Figure 51) will help. The muscles of the lower abdomen become really involved on the word "am." In any case, the second word beginning with a vowel must be "thought" right into the hard palate.

CONSONANTS LEAD OUT THE VOWEL

"The consonant is the 'lead out' for the vowel and is of vital importance.''[2] When the consonant is done correctly it is a wonderful lead out. If done incorrectly, a consonant will block the vowel. The singer should feel the involvement of the mask on all consonants. He should always remember that when he allows the "hook" muscle to be involved with consonants, the consonants will be more sharply pronounced and the breath will go farther to sustain a longer phrase. One should never bang or press any of the consonants. Consonants are all sung gently, but with the "hook" muscle giving them energy and clarity.

An "m," for instance, if done incorrectly, will pull the upper lip down and pull the vowel out of the resonating spaces over the hard palate and the nasopharynx. The lips should *never* be pinched or pressed on any consonant. They should feel very loose. For example, on the word "mother," the lips feel very soft on the "m" and one has the sensation of the space that we found on the "preh" exercises, using "pruh," the same sound as "muh." If the upper lip presses when the "m" is sung, the voice is pulled out of the nasopharyngeal area.

The double "m," as in the German word "Himmel," requires that the lips be together as in a humming sound, slightly buzzing. The lips must be free enough to vibrate, not pinched. The double "m" must be sounded longer than a single "m" sound, and it must be *voiced*.

When speaking a "b" we ordinarily pull the upper lip down. When singing, we do not dare bring that upper lip down without a feeling of air underneath it and a feeling of a loose upper lip. When the lip is loose it *allows* the tone to feel as though it goes up into the nasopharynx or hard and soft palate areas. When the "b" is pulled down by the upper lip, it loses the "ping" in its quality.

The same holds true for the consonant "p." When the "p" presses or pulls the upper lip down and the vowel, such as "ah" in "part" follows it, the "ah" sound goes to "aw" as in "awful." If used incorrectly, the upper lip will change the "shape" of any vowel sound following the consonant and therefore the vowel will not be the pure vowel that it should be.

If one tries to say "mah" with a feeling of air under the upper lip, he will get a pure "ah" sound. If he presses or pulls down the upper lip and sings "mah" it will sound "maw." When the corners of the mouth are stretched wide, the sound will be "white," or too bright an "ah" sound. The way to assure the correct "b" or "p" consonant, then, is to have the upper lip in a *normal position* and feel the air underneath.

The "l" can be a problem; the answer to that is that the tongue and jaw *always* move together on the "l," and the tip of the tongue is wide and soft behind the lower front teeth.

---

[2]Ibid.

If the jaw stays down and the tongue goes up, there is a pull at the root of the tongue muscle. It can be felt by placing the hands just below the jaw bone, a little in front of the jaw hinge, and dropping the jaw, keeping it open and singing "lah, lah, lah." One feels a muscular action there at the root of the tongue. When the jaw and the tongue go together, there is no pull in that area of the throat and the tone quality being produced is much better than the one produced with the tongue up and the jaw down.

In the German, such as in "Liebe" (love), the "l" is voiced. In order to voice the "l" without tightening the throat, the tongue should feel wide at the tip and vibrating as the "l" is sung. The tongue must *never* be tight or pressed while singing the "l."

When a word *ends* with an "l," *the jaw should come up as the word is finished*; otherwise, the tone is hard to release. The double "l" as in the Italian "bella" (beautiful) must have the tongue and jaw coming up together; one goes into the "l" immediately, actually vocalizing the consonant. I emphasize that the tongue must remain *wide at the tip and soft and that the jaw and tongue move together*.

The "d" is sung with exactly the same principle as the "l."

What does one do when he has an "l," for instance on "laugh" or "love," at the top of an interval? He should put the "l" on the *bottom* of the interval, leaving the jaw and the tongue together. The jaw should come up as he is singing the "l," and it should swing open as he sings the *vowel* that follows the "l."

On a "t," the tip of the tongue is wide and soft, and there is always a puff of air after its enunciation. Other than that, it involves the same principle as the "l" and the "d." I want to emphasize the importance of that little *puff of air* that must go with the "t" to obtain sharp diction.

The "g" many times grabs at the back of the tongue. It must *never* be thought of as being any further back than the first upper molar tooth. The tongue is wide, touching the lower front teeth, the tip of the tongue lies loosely against the lower front teeth, and the back of the tongue is arched and touching the roof of the mouth.

A little behind center, but still on the hard palate, the consonant "j" is also in front of the first upper molar tooth.

"F" and "v" are wonderful "lead-out consonants" for vowels if done correctly. On both of these consonants, one should feel a very soft lower lip with the teeth touching it lightly. The "f" and "v" are wonderful to help establish that inside smile of which we have spoken so many times before in this book. The lower lip is in a normal wide position on both consonants. Never bite or press the lower lip to form them. It is always done gently. Air flows through the "f" as in the word "fine." The "v" is voiced, and one feels a slight vibration of the lips against the teeth.

On the "r" which ends a word such as "her," one should always think of "huh" and allow the "r" to be slightly flipped with the tip of the tongue. The "r" will invariably want to go to the back of the tongue if one does not let the tip of the tongue flip it. On "r" before a consonant, such as "world," one should think of the "pruh" spot (Figure 33) and eliminate the "r" completely. Think "wuh"! For "earth," think "uhth" like "pruh."

The tip of the tongue is wide for both voiced "th" ("this") and unvoiced "th" ("think"), and the tongue lies between the teeth.

A major block to clear diction is the all too common habit of dropping consonants. Consonants must have a long enough duration for the listener to be able to understand the consonant; this is especially important in the case of consonants that begin words, so that the consonants will have an opportunity to correctly "seat" the vowels, or "lead out" the vowels that follow. Another place where it is crucial to have a consonant with duration is in emotionally charged words where the duration of the consonant can add the necessary emotional coloring. (One should remember, of course, that if a word begins with a consonant, it should usually precede the beat so that the vowel will be on the beat; otherwise the singing will sound lethargic.)

Some consonants have the potential of being "pressed" if sung incorrectly; they should therefore be sung with less duration to take care of this problem.

CONSONANTS WITH DURATION–VOICED

L   — Tip of tongue wide and soft and against lower front teeth

M   — Lips soft and buzzing (mask strong, not pulled down)

N   — Tip of tongue against upper front teeth, soft—*do not press the tongue*

NG— Tongue feels as though it is arching against the hard palate

R   — American "r": Arch of the tongue is in front of first molar tooth, tip of tongue forward. Flipped "r": tongue flipped against upper gum ridge

TH — ("That"): Soft tip of tongue between teeth

V   — Wide lower lip; teeth not pressing

W   — (Vowel)—"oo"

Y   — (Vowel)—"ih"

Z   — Air vibrates through front teeth

CONSONANTS WITH DURATION–UNVOICED

F — "Wide" teeth softly touching the lower lip, lower lip normally wide

H — Aspirant—One should not allow too much air to escape on this "breath stealer"

S — (C=S) Breath flowing between front teeth

SS — Breath flowing between front teeth

TH — ("Through") Tip of tongue between front teeth but not beyond the lips

CONSONANTS WITH LESS DURATION–VOICED

B — Air should be felt under the upper lip; the lip should *not* be pressed down but be feeling soft

D — Soft tip of tongue behind upper front teeth

G — Felt no further back than the first molar tooth

J — (DG) See comments for D and G

K — Soft palate involved

CONSONANTS WITH LESS DURATION–UNVOICED

C — (C=K)

CH — (Tch) Puff of air through the teeth

P — Air should be felt under an *unpressed* upper lip

Q — (Q=KW)

T — A puff of air should be felt after it

X — (X=KS)

KEY POINTS TO REMEMBER

1. Each vowel has its own "seat" and is formed by involving the lips, oral cavity, nasopharynx, oropharynx, and breath support.

2. Diphthongs and glides have their own rules which should be studied carefully.

3. Whenever a phrase begins with a vowel, there should be a snuffing-up sensation followed by a jaw swing into the tone.

4. When two vowels come together, there must be a jaw swing between them.

5. Two consonants coming together between words often demand an ''air pause'' between them.

6. Consonants lead a vowel out of the mouth.

10

LEARNING TO SING
THE VOCAL TEXT

It is a major achievement when the singer can incorporate the principles and techniques he has been learning into the literature he is singing and use them effectively and correctly. When he works with the exercises in the context of literature, it is easy to use the anatomy involved in correctly singing the vocal text. Learning to sing using sensations learned through using the exercises given in this book will allow the vocal literature its best chance to be sung with a noninterrupted vocal line.

The singer should begin singing literature early in his studies. It is important that the literature should lie in his middle range, since that range should be technically secure before extending the upper or lower ranges of the voice. The music should also be flowing so that his still weak pull-ups do not get pulled down in a position which does not have an inside smile.

I feel that the early Italian classical literature is the most appropriate music for training a "beginning voice." It is advisable that the classical singer study at least two languages other than his own so that he can develop a feeling for the singing of different vocal texts. Knowledge of a foreign language (spoken and/or written) is invaluable in singing; it is *imperative* for a concert or operatic career!

There are excellent collections of Italian art songs published by G. Schirmer, Inc.[1] which should be considered an integral part of the singer's

---

[1]*Anthology of Italian Song of the Seventeenth and Eighteenth Centuries,* Book 1, Vol. 290, (New York, G. Schirmer, Inc., 1926)

Anthology of Italian Song of the Seventeenth and Eighteenth Centuries, Book 2, Vol. 291, (New York, G. Schirmer, Inc., 1926)

Twenty-Four Italian Songs and Arias of the Seventeenth and Eighteenth Century, (Medium high voice), Vol. 1722, (New York, G. Schirmer, Inc., 1948)

Twenty-Four Italian Songs and Arias of the Seventeenth and Eighteenth Centuries, (Medium low voice), Vol. 1723, (New York, G. Schirmer, Inc., 1948)

library. Songs and arias from these books should be chosen during the second or third lesson. The student should then memorize them as quickly as possible. The study of the song and the application of exercises to the vocal text can then be worked on with greater concentration, giving the student a good idea of just how the technique described in this text actually works in practice.

There is a correct way in which to proceed when learning to sing the vocal text of any song or aria, be it written in English, Italian, German, French or any other language.

The most important aspect in learning a text is knowing exactly what the text means and not just understanding the general thrust of the words. *Each song or aria should be translated word for word* and the translation written in the music above each word to which it applies.

There is an excellent book available which will help in the translation of the early Italian songs and arias entitled *Word by Word Translations of Songs and Arias* (Volume II).[2] This book is of great value in that it gives the direct literal, not paraphrased, translation of many songs and arias; this volume also should be part of the singer's music library. (Volume I of the same edition provides translations of German and French texts[3] and likewise should be in the singer's library.)

After the singer has translated the text and written the translation above the original language in the music, he should then learn to speak the text phonetically and in rhythm.

When the text is finally learned and the student is able to speak it freely in the original language (with the translation in mind), he should then work on the music itself and learn the melodic line. After having learned the melody, the student can then put the original text to the music and *only then should the song actually be sung*.

At that point, the song should be brought to the lesson so that the voice teacher can demonstrate the technique that will help the student to best sing the text, showing the student the technical principles involved in combining the written language with a musical line. Should the student learn the song technically incorrectly, it is difficult to reverse his impressions; it is most important that the student learn to sing the song or aria *technically correctly* in the beginning.

THE ROLE OF VOCAL AND DRAMATIC COACHES

The voice teacher will have to help the singer with the beginning instruction in the pronunciation of the language (particularly if the singer has not had a

---

[2] Arthur Schoep and Daniel Harris, *Word by Word Translations of Songs and Arias*, Vol. II, (Metuchen, N.J., Scarecrow Press, 1972)

[3] Berton Coffin, Werner Singer and Pierre Dellatre, *Word by Word Translations of Songs and Arias*, Vol. I, (New York, Scarecrow Press, 1966).

background in that language). When the singer is far enough advanced in his study of technique, he should then begin study with a vocal coach who can also instruct him in languages and assist in directing him (along with the teacher of voice) in the proper literature to sing, based on his vocal timbre, range, and capabilities. (Determining a singer's capabilities should be left to the sensitive teacher of voice and the coach. A singer's ambitions at a given time may far exceed his capabilities, and he must not try to exceed his limits if he is to progress vocally.)

Coaching also teaches the singer how to interpret the piece and how to set the moods which best suit the text. It is important to note, however, that expression of the text cannot be learned entirely through coaching. As very ably expressed by F.E. Miller, "No coaching, however admirable, can ever result in anything better than imitation; interpretation is creative and artistic only when achieved by the voice itself."[4]

It is important that the singer have a solid technique from which the coach can develop his ability to express the song; bad singing technique ultimately makes the singer *more* aware of his deficiencies rather than allowing him to reach a goal of expression of thought through singing vocal literature.

The last, but certainly not the least, step in achieving vocal artistry, is to go to a fine dramatic coach. When I learned my first complete role, Santuzza, in "Cavalleria Rusticana," I still was not doing all I felt could be done with it. I attended the Stanislavsky School of Dramatics and worked on the dramatic qualities of the role with the drama coach. The role came alive!

When I learned the role of Isolde in "Tristan und Isolde," I was being coached in drama by Dino Yannopoulos of the Metropolitan Opera Company. As soon as I finished the blocking of the role, a new dimension came into my voice! When I was directing the Opera Workshop at University of Redlands (California), the same thing happened with every student in those productions. All their voices took on more depth and more meaning after the dramatic aspect was worked into the role.

One should *never* try to block a role that is not completely memorized or musically and vocally well prepared. If a singer is not prepared, he can tear down a lot of that vocal line that has been so carefully developed. Remember, "one thing at a time" and "make haste slowly."

TECHNIQUE FIRST AND THEN EXPRESSION

The final polishing of a song or aria will come only after correct technique has been made part of the piece. Polishing comes with phrasing and coloring (see Chapter 11); but phrasing and coloring, and learning how to do them

---

[4]Frank E. Miller, *Vocal Art Science,* (New York, G. Schirmer, Inc., 1922)

masterfully, are more advanced studies in vocal technique and should not be concentrated upon during the first part of a singer's technical education.

A natural development in a singer's vocal technique will eventually allow the instructor, as well as the singer himself, to know when the student is ready to begin a study of phrasing and coloring. The most important thing when adding these new dimensions to singing comes from knowing the text and its translations thoroughly, coupled with practicing the singing of the text using the techniques which will help form each word (its vowels and consonants) in the context of the musical line.

When consistency in "floating" words on the musical line is attained, the student can easily control the vocal line, and phrase and color it in order to convey the message. The word "bella" (in Italian), for example, means "beautiful," while the word "schrecklich" (in German) is translated into English as "terrible." These words are absolutely opposite in meaning and require individual colors. If they are sung so that one seems to have the meaning of the other, or, as more often happens, with no meaning at all, the singer obviously does not know the meaning of his text. Knowledge of what the word actually means and application of coloring appropriate to it will give the correct interpretation of what the song is saying. The ability to obtain various vocal colors comes from complete control of the technique used to obtain it and should only be practiced when the student has reached that level of study.

KEY POINTS TO REMEMBER

1. A beginning student should start, within just a few weeks, working on the classical early Italian literature.

2. Every song in a foreign language should be translated word for word into the singer's native tongue.

3. When the singer progresses to the point where it would be valuable, he should work with both a vocal coach and a dramatic coach.

4. The vocal technique of a particular song should always be mastered before concentrating on interpretation of the text.

11

TESTED AND EFFECTIVE PERFORMANCE TECHNIQUE

On the day of a concert or performance of any kind, the singer should be quiet and stay away from conversation with anyone. He should write letters or read to keep his mind off the music to be performed.

When a singer reaches the level at which he is giving programs, he must, first of all, be concerned about the first impression which he makes when he walks onto the stage.

First of all, the body should be erect—the arms should hang loosely at the sides, never swinging too wide for one's body proportions, nor should they be held stiffly at the side of the body. The singer should walk with a good "zip" or authority in his step, coming on stage with confidence.

When the applause begins, he should turn his head slightly toward the audience, giving them a big smile, never "bobbing" the head toward them. He should not start his actual bow until he gets into the curve of the piano. The bow depends on the amount of the applause. If it is a big ovation, the bow can be deeper, but, regardless of the amount of the applause, the artist should always recognize it with a bow, *after* he is at the piano. He should have a feeling of humility as he bows.

One should bow by letting the eyes look downward first, then feeling as though the forehead follows the eyes, allowing the head to follow. The neck should arch slightly, the shoulders following, and then bending at the waistline. The body feels as though it rolls over gradually (never quickly) from the waist. When one comes back up, the back comes first, *then* the neck and then the head. The eyes and head should never come up first. This gives a very bad line to the body.

After singing the group of songs, or an aria, the singer turns toward the accompanist and acknowledges him with a smile. The accompanist stands and bows (keeping his hand off the piano) in the same way as the singer does. The singer then turns to the audience and bows again. If the singer is male and the accompanist female, the singer leads off, the accompanist following until they get to the wings of the stage. Here the male singer steps back and the female accompanist goes ahead of the singer.

If the appearance of the artist is at an informal function where he must announce his numbers, *his speaking voice should be completely supported,* the same as when he is singing. The names of the selections to be sung should be spoken very articulately.

The accompanist should never begin without knowing that the singer is ready to begin. There are different ways of giving this signal. I prefer the singer's looking down and then lifting his eyes and head to give the signal to begin, rather than nodding to the accompanist.

After each selection is sung, the singer and the accompanist should "hold the mood" of the song or aria until the pedal is lifted and *no sound* is coming from the piano.

When standing before an audience, it is important to look beyond the audience to the back row, keeping the head comparatively level. One should not look up into the balcony; this makes one look wall-eyed as the audience can only see the whites of the eyes. If the audience is in a big circle, the singer's head should be kept toward the center; it may be turned very slightly left or right. If turned too far in either direction, it will cut out the audience to the side of the head.

One should not wear eye glasses on stage. There is always a glare on the lens when behind the footlights. This breaks the audience contact with the performer's eyes. The eyes should be expressive, helping set the mood of the song, and they cannot be seen behind a glare. Audience contact is most important!

Earlier in this text I have said that singing is an athletic event—and so it is. An excellent book has recently been published called *Maximum Performance.*[1] I recommend it highly to all singers.

Stage fright, to a certain degree, is imperative. (I prefer to call it *eagerness.*) Without it one would become a "flat" performer. "Performance *requires* tension."[2] This *eagerness* causes the adrenalin to flow through one's body. It "dilates the vessels of the skeletal muscles, letting more blood into them to help them with their work."[3] The artist must have just enough tension or *eagerness* in his body to keep him up and going, but not so much as to "tie him up." This eagerness for a good performance is not to be confused with what I call "stage fright."

---

[1]Lawrence E. Morehouse, and Leonard Gross, *Maximum Performance,* (New York, Simon & Schuster, 1977)
[2]Ibid.
[3]Ibid.

STAGE FRIGHT

Three things cause stage fright: not being musically secure, not being vocally secure, and egotism. If one is insecure *musically* with even one number in a recital, that insecurity will cause nervousness throughout the entire recital. That selection should be omitted from the program. A recital should be memorized at least a whole semester, preferably a whole year, before it is to be sung.

If one is *vocally* insecure with any number on a recital, that number should be omitted as well. The singer must know and feel security in his vocal production before performing anything publicly. This does not mean that he must wait until he is vocally *perfect,* but he should always come away from a public appearance with a good feeling, not a feeling of having done badly. This is why short appearances in a student recital, singing only one group of songs, can be a very important part of one's growth as a singer.

Now, what is *egotism*? The singer is thinking about what someone out in the audience is thinking about him. This will always cause nervousness. *The mind should be centered on the message of the song to be sung,* the moods, the music, and how that message will be given. At the very moment before a performance, the singer should have prepared himself well, musically and vocally. From that point on he is simply a channel through which the music is flowing.

The singer should never choose music that goes beyond what he can do vocally at that stage of his development. So often, young singers begin singing arias which are way beyond them vocally. This is never good for the voice; the music will not be sung well and will only cause nervousness in the mind of that young performer.

WITHOUT A GOOD TECHNIQUE THERE IS NO INTERPRETATION

When a singer has mastered the techniques described in this book, is capable of implementing the basic principles, and can easily apply these principles while singing, then the art of *coloring and phrasing* the vocal text can be easily learned. In order to present the text in its most effective and expressive mood, the singer must color and phrase the music intelligently so that the subject matter, mood, and attitude of the piece can be communicated to the audience. A singer who has mastered the major portion of the techniques outlined in this book will have the ability to execute *all* vocal colors.

"Vocal colors" can be described as those tones produced by opening or closing or combining different resonating spaces to produce a given emotion or effect (love, hate, sarcasm, or narration). When a composer sets a text carefully, he is aware of the various vocal colors that he wishes to bring out in that text as well as the potentials and limitations of the human voice.

HOW DO WE GET THESE COLORS?

A good example of literature needing many colors is Schubert's *Der Erlkönig*. This song includes a narrator, a child, a desperate father, and Death—all requiring different colors from the singer.

The narrator requires a color that is impersonal and well-balanced, a "mixed tone." The voice will be felt in the entire oral cavity. The tone will be focused front with the back spaces open.

Imitating a child's voice will demand more headiness where the only space used will be that up over the hard palate and soft palate. The child in *Der Erlkönig,* for example, is filled with fear. The voice should have a breathiness in it at the beginning, achieved by cutting out the resonant feeling in the voice and the focus. Later on, the child becomes frantic as he hears the Erl King.

When the singer "becomes" the father, he expresses concern, and in doing so there is a slight increase in intensity in the tone which in itself changes the color. The father's response to the child's fearful questions is one of assurance—a warm, dark color. This is obtained by a complete opening of the back spaces and oral cavity including a feeling of resonance in the chest with the text sung right into the teeth. (Schubert wrote this to lie in the low range of the voice to help get these colors. A fine composer knows which ranges to draw upon to draw out the colors to express his text.)

The next color is an enticing one which is used by Death. It lies in a higher range and is sung in a very heady voice *all front,* with the spaces open under the mask but not at the back. The child's next voice is one of great fright, almost a crying tone. This is obtained by letting the childlike tone resonate in the nasopharynx (with no feeling of the back spaces being open). This does not have breathiness, however, and is more focused.

The father answers in a pleading tone, warm again, and involving the back spaces *and* the front spaces. It is higher in range than the first time he spoke and therefore has a little more bite in the tone.

Then Death speaks, trying again to entice the child with a sweet lullaby. This is done by allowing the tones to be heady, but they lie higher so there is just a little more bite in the tone. The back spaces are still kept open, however, to give warmth to the tone. When the child speaks again it is still higher in pitch; the highest pitch allows the color again to change by becoming more intense. The father then answers, still with a warm tone and the pitch lowered.

Death then speaks with a very threatening tone, right in the nasopharynx, cutting off the back spaces. It is *almost* a nasal tone at this point. Then the child speaks at a higher pitch level, almost screaming to his father. This is all front, but it also uses the back spaces in order to get the dramatic impact required. The father's tone after this is one of shuddering, emphasized by the German word "grausets" (shudders).

One can see very vividly how the different ranges which are employed assist the singer greatly in getting the colors that the composer wishes into the voice.

The tempo changes of the music also are a clue to the colors. When the father is frantic, the tempo accelerates and the voice is all in the teeth, giving a different color. At the end of the song, the father's grief is expressed with the voice fully open and in the low range of the voice.

A word of warning: The emotions should never get ahead of the voice. ". . . excessive emotion ruins a performance."[4] How early in life did I learn this lesson. I sang *Der Erlkönig* in my senior recital in college. I was so "into the emotion of it" by the time I sang the last line "das Kind war tot" (the child was dead), tears were running down my cheeks but practically no tone was coming from my throat.

The singing of art songs is, in many ways, more difficult in technique and coloring requirements than the art form of opera. Often what happens in three hours in an opera must be accomplished in three minutes in an art song. Usually, the protagonists and antagonists in the songs are more difficult to distinguish, and thus subtle phrasing and tone coloring, and more vivid use of dynamics must be employed in order to make the characters and their personalities appear more strongly and realistically. Usually, the colors of tones describe in sound the setting, and they display the character of the person(s) within the setting. It is very difficult to master the art of coloring, ornamenting and phrasing without studying and perfecting the basic principles described in the preceding chapters.

THE WARM AND/OR LOVING TONE COLOR

In the aria, "Ave Maria" from Verdi's *Otello,* Desdemona is on her knees praying. The aria begins in the lower part of the range with a recitative. The recitative is a form of speaking on pitch and demands the clarity and articulation found in a forward position but with the back spaces open and a feeling of strong support from the sternum. This particular recitative expresses warmth so the back spaces must be open.

---

[4]Ibid.

As the recitative proceeds to the aria, ascending from E' flat to C'' (Figure 21), the feeling of the focus moves from the lower teeth (lower range) to the head (middle range). The back continues to remain open, the soft palate is arched and the inside smile present. As the word "prega" is approached, the mask comes into play on the low note to prepare for the C.

The aria is then sung in "head voice." It is a light, spun tone as opposed to a tone having a passionate quality. The head tone is produced by allowing the tone to feel as though it goes back up over the soft palate, giving a feeling as though the sound is actually resonating in the head, above the hard palate and soft palate. The tone feels as though it travels upward into the skull and spins around there without involving the mouth or chest. The tone can be described as angelic or pure but the breath support must be as strong as that required for a fortissimo tone.

At the end of the aria, the word "Ave" is also sung in head voice ascending from A' flat to high A'' flat. The "a" is sung on the lower note followed by sounding the "v" on the same lower note and releasing the "e" sound on the top pitch. This interval will always be easier to sing if one thinks of putting the consonant "v" on the *bottom* of the interval and the "e" at the top with the jaw swinging.

THE PANTS ROLE

The pants role was used many years ago by such composers as Rossini, Bellini and Donizetti and was sung by women taking the role of male characters in the opera.

The mezzo voice was usually used for these roles. The deeper, more dynamic voice colors were used because they represented (in color) the sound of the youthful male voice. The vocal scoring for these singers was usually very ornamented, so it is important that vocal technique be learned well so that the ornaments can be performed effortlessly.

The fast moving runs, trills, mordents, turns and portamentos so characteristic of the operatic roles of this historical period should be performed effortlessly, lightly, and with great intensity, especially in the case of the pants role, in order to give the male personality a youthful agility combined with strength of character. When the soft palate is strong, the mask and the jaw in balance, the upper lip strong and involved, and the breath support correct, these ornaments will come easily. The vocal color of the pants role is dark, yet it has a very definite focus in the tone (more than the ordinary female voice would have). It is obtained by singing into the teeth and the nasal cavity, supported by a feeling of strength from the sternum.

LULLABY FROM "SONGS AND DANCES OF DEATH" BY MUSSORGSKY

This song involves three characters, yet it is sung by one person. As in the Schubert *Erlkönig* described earlier, each of the three characters must have a distinct difference in tone quality; i.e., a difference in the *color* of the tone. The singer must be able to precisely call on different tone colors in order to go in and out of the three different roles. Through the use of technique and the phrasing of the vocal line, the subtle as well as obvious differences in personalities of the three roles can be easily sung.

The three characters are the narrator, Death and the mother. The narrator tells the tale of a conflict between the mother of a dying child and Death (personified). The narrator should take on a mixed tone, the front and back spaces employed, a normal singing voice with inflections here and there indicating the spoken dialogue. The voice coloring should be warm, flowing and free—rather neutral.

The role of Death should be sung with the tones feeling as though they are lying in the chest, being darker than the narrator's. These tones are not sung in the chest, but rather should be colored by use of a wide opened throat. The tones are not sung in head voice but should be shaded with dark overtones and should harbor depth and power. This requires a feeling of strong support from the sternum, a completely open oral cavity, and the front and back pull-ups in balance.

The mother is rather hysterical in character and at times full of hate. Her tones should "sit" forward in the nasal cavity. The tones should be pointed and vibrant with a sense of hysteria, of great activity and anxiety. This is accomplished by using the nasal cavity exclusively. The notes should be attacked more readily and the text sung in a more hurried and agitated manner, unlike the steadfast and self-assured presence of Death.

It is very difficult to sing a song such as this in such varying degrees of intensity and vocal coloring. For one voice type to present three different characters through extensive phrasing, that voice must be capable of mastering very advanced techniques as well as be extremely flexible.

SCHUMANN'S "FRAUENLIEBE UND LEBEN"

Perhaps another color which should be mentioned concerns the ability of a mature woman to sing with the color of a sixteen-year-old, such as *Frauenliebe und Leben* (A Woman's Life and Love) by Schumann.

The cycle begins with a young girl who is very naive. The tone should have a breathiness, which means cutting out most of the resonance. In the second song, a little more resonance can be used and, as the cycle develops and her child has been born, there is a maturity that comes into the color of the woman's voice which begins to use the resonating spaces more fully. By the end of the cycle, where she has lost her husband, she has become still more mature. In the last song, which is written in the lower range of the voice, all of the resonating spaces including the chest resonance, the oral cavity, and the hard and soft palate spaces become involved. In this cycle we have a vivid example of how one gets "colors" from one extreme to the other.

This is what makes a singer an interesting singer: *To know how to get a particular color into the voice whenever it is desired.*

CHARACTER ROLES

The Emperor in "The Mikado" by Gilbert and Sullivan

The Emperor is a pompous and sinister character who says and sings a lot of mean and nasty things. In order to portray the character authentically, the singer must use certain techniques which will give the sung line a theme of evil and ruthlessness. In order to do this, the character should speak the tones directed to the front of the face, up over the hard palate and soft palate. To accomplish this, the "mee-oh" exercise (Figure 69) and the "preh" exercise (Figure 33) should be used to activate the "pull-up" muscles of the inside upper lip and nasal cavity. The tone will then "sit" in these spaces and have the desired nasty sound. The tone is pointed and concentrated, and will have much "front" in its core, with chest but very little mixed voice. Of course, as the dialogue calls for it, mixtures of tones going in and out of nasal and chest and mixed tones can be used to give great effect and real character to the personality.

The nastier the character must become, the further front the tone should "sit" until it is *completely* nasal in quality. As the tone becomes further front, the spaces in the back of the mouth are cut off from resonance, and the space used for resonance is that of the nasal cavity. Of course, nothing should be felt in the throat. When all of the basic principles are applied, the use of the nasal tone can be very effective and not at all physically harmful to the vocal mechanism.

The Witch in "Hansel and Gretel" by Humperdinck

The Witch is again a character of evil intentions and must be portrayed as such. The biting, cold and evil tones sung by this character must be positioned frontally, in the nasal cavity. The entire role is sung in this manner with the upper lip pulling up all the while. The mask should be strong, but the inside smile and the soft palate are never activated throughout the role. There is absolutely no back space present in the tone; the tone is shrill, striking the bones in the hard palate and up against the nasal septum.

THE BELTING OR "BROADWAY" TONE

The ''mee-oh'' exercise (Figure 69) and ''preh'' exercises (Figure 33) should be used to attain the belting tone or that sound which is termed ''Broadway.'' The *hard* (guttural) rock sound is very injurious to the throat and therefore I do not deal with it at all. The belting tone is the sound produced by singers who wish to project a big sound without hurting the vocal mechanism.

It is important, when the student is beginning to use this technique, that he not *try* to produce a big sound. *Never* push the voice. Let it grow normally. The singer will feel a great deal of the tone hitting the hard palate area, and, in the beginning, a whiny unpleasant sound will probably result; but, with consistent and careful practice, the singer develops an awareness of the spaces which create the belting tone and the strength of the sound grows.

Caution: Be sure the tone is being made in the nasal cavity without any restriction in the throat. The tone is sung into the hard palate, through the nose. There is a feeling of support from the sternum mixed with use of the nasal spaces, because the belting range is usually in the low and low-middle ranges. It is important not to try to carry the belting tone too high when it is uncomfortable in the throat. As the skill of the singer develops in sensing these different areas of resonance, the ability of ''varying'' the colors will be accomplished.

The developing of the belting technique will always improve the voice so that even the operatic voice develops beautifully as long as the person continues to work on his operatic literature. The focus that this technique develops demands complete support of the lower abdominal area, a sensation all singers should have.

****

The following quotations have had a great impact on my teaching. It was a relief to know that, when a student and I had worked very hard on achieving varying vocal colors, and the result was not all that we wished, it was possible that the physiological makeup of the student precluded our achieving the desired results.

As Gustav Kobbe said in his ''Note'' to Dr. Miller's book, *The Voice*:

> Above all, Dr. Miller, while convinced that the tones of the vocal scale require, for their correct emission, subtly corresponding changes of adjustment in the vocal organs, utterly rejects anything like a deliberate or

conscious attempt on the singer's part to bring about these adjustments. He holds that they should occur automatically (or subconsciously) as the result, in very rare instances, of supreme natural gifts, in others as a spontaneous sequence to properly developed artistry.[5]

In Chapter I of the same volume, Dr. Miller explains,

The proper physiological basis for a singing method having been laid, something else, something highly important, remains to be superimposed. Voice is physical. But everything that colors voice, charging it with emotion, giving it its peculiar quality and making it different from other voices, is largely, although not wholly, the result of a psychical control—a control not exercised mysteriously from without, like Svengali's over Trilby, but by the singer himself from within. Every singer is his own mesmerist, or he has mistaken his vocation. For while voice is a physical manifestation, its "atmosphere," its emotional thrill and charm, is a psychical one—the result of the individual's thought and feeling, acting unconsciously or, better still, subsonsciously, on that physical thing, the voice.

Between the two, however, between mind and body, there lies, like a borderland of fancy, yet most real, the nervous system, crossed and recrossed by the most delicate, the most sensitive filaments ever spun, filaments that touch, caress, or permeate each and every muscle concerned in voice production, calling them into play with the rapidity of mental telegraphy. Over this network of nerves the mind, or—if you prefer to call it so—the artistic sense, sends its messages, and it is the nerves and muscles working in harmony that results in a correct production of the voice. So important, indeed, is the cooperation of the nervous system, that it is a question whether the whole psychology of song may not be referred to it—whether the degree of emotional thrill, in different voices, may not be the result of greater or less sensitiveness in the nervous system of different singers. This might explain why some very beautiful voices lack emotional quality. In such singers the physical action of the vocal organs and all of the resonance cavities of the head may be perfect, but the nerves are not sufficiently sensitive to the emotion which the song is intended to express, and so fail to carry it to the voice.[6]

It takes many elements in developing a vocal artist. Commitment almost always ranks first, the vocal instrument second, musicianship very near to the first two, then come personal appearance (charisma), and inner drive. Every singer does not have to become an opera singer or a Broadway star to give joy, and in so giving, get joy in return.

---

[5]Frank E. Miller, *The Voice,* (New York, G. Schirmer, Inc., 1910)
[6]Ibid.

KEY POINTS TO REMEMBER

1. The singer should be very conscious of his appearance on stage and constantly remind himself of
   - the correct way to walk on stage
   - the correct way to bow
   - how to leave the stage
   - his appearance on stage
   - how to use his body, head, and face most effectively to interpret his song
2. Stage fright is attributable to
   - being musically insecure
   - being vocally insecure
   - egotism
3. Vocal colors can be achieved only after the mastery of vocal techniques, and those tones are produced by opening or closing or combining different resonating spaces.

12

TECHNIQUES AND EXERCISES THAT PRODUCE
DYNAMIC AND EXCITING
CHORAL PERFORMANCES

Choral singing should be a great experience for the singer, the listener, and the director. Too often, however, it is a frustrating experience, especially for the director. It is important in choral singing to know how to get the particular sound one desires at the time one wishes to use it for dynamic, dramatic, and expressive purposes. This task can be especially difficult when working with untrained singers. The first step toward this goal is always a basic understanding of the vocal instrument and principles of vocal production. The choral director is in part responsible for the vocal health of the choir and should always encourage good singing habits.

It is very important, I think, to remember that, along with technique, a director must keep a happy feeling in the choir. "All work and no play makes Jack a dull boy," and the same it is in our choral rehearsals. It is very important that *enthusiasm* is kept in rehearsal and not just the drudgery of pounding in notes and rhythm.

WARM-UPS ARE IMPERATIVE

One purpose of the warm-up is to get the choir members into a good frame of mind to sing their best. It is important to maintain the singer's self-esteem. A director should never ridicule or imitate poor sounds in a derogatory way. The mistakes a choir member makes are honest ones because he does not *know,* not because he does not care.

It is also important that a choral group be "bodily alive." Warm-ups are imperative! In the process of warming up one's singers, the first areas to consider are the big muscles of the body—the abdominal area, torso, lungs—to get the blood circulating through the body. Following general body warm-ups, one is ready to warm up the voice. This may be accomplished through vocalises which warm the tiny muscles that control the vocal cords and the muscles which open the spaces of the nasal cavity and pharyngeal area. As an organist, a pianist or a violinist warms up the fingers before playing, so too a singer must warm up the body and voice.

The immediate result of such warm-up techniques will be a choir with longer endurance and better tone quality.

Windmill Exercise

The first thing to do, if the space of the room will permit, is to spread the group out so that they may be able to swing their arms rapidly in a circle in front of their bodies. The knees should always be flexed and the body bent slightly forward from the waist. Each singer swings one arm in a clockwise position across the front of the body and up over the head making a complete circle, inhaling and exhaling once with each swing of the arm. This is done six times with each arm. One should remember, as he is inhaling, to allow the breath to come through the nose and to always exhale through the mouth. When one finishes this exercise, the body feels very tingly as the blood circulates rapidly throughout the body.

The Rag Doll

The second exercise which I like to do is the "rag doll." In this exercise, one simply lets the body fall forward from the waist, keeping the knees flexed. If possible, the tips of the fingers should touch the floor. The head and the neck should not be held stiff, but should be allowed to drop also. One should feel as though the spine is unraveling. While remaining in this position, one should bounce easily from the waist, then take a deep breath, feeling as though the ribs in the back are expanding. Then the body should be raised *easily,* retaining the breath which was just taken in, and, after assuming a standing position, the singer should exhale very easily, allowing the abdomen to come in on the exhalation. The chest remains wide, without dropping at all. One should never attempt to *hold* the chest up, but should simply *let it remain high and wide across the front.*

Shoulder Exercises

The next exercise deals with tension in the back of the shoulders and the back of the neck. The shoulders should be lifted up to the ears and dropped. This should be done three times in a very relaxed manner. After completing this exercise, one should stand with the shoulders wide and roll the head clockwise three times. After a brief pause, it should be rolled in the opposite direction three times. The shoulders should be wide and the back of the neck should be very straight. (The shoulders should feel as though they are on a coat hanger.)

In the next shoulder exercise, both shoulders should be pulled back until the shoulder blades touch—pulled gently—never with a jerk. After the shoulder blades have pinched together in the back, they should be allowed to return to a normal position while keeping the chest wide. (They should never be pulled so far front that the chest collapses.) (Figure 16, p. 60)

This exercise is done three times in this way and the fourth time the shoulders are pulled back and down. During this exercise the neck remains straight (never thrust forward) and the shoulders move straight back and are never lifted. One feels a stretching of the muscles at the back of the neck and shoulder area. By keeping the knees flexed, one also feels a lengthening or stretching of the spine.

Sometimes it is impossible to do this exercise correctly at first, especially for people with "rounded shoulders." An attempt should still be made, however, to pull the shoulder blades back as far as possible. It is very important to remember that one should never jerk the shoulders in this exercise. It is a *stretching* exercise.

Torso Exercise

In the first exercise for warming up the torso area, the hands should be placed on the waist. The body should bend slightly forward at the waist, the knees flexed. The upper torso should be rotated from the waist, first to the left and then to the right. This should be done twice, always keeping the body rolling from the waist. During this exercise, the head and the neck should be very relaxed.

The singer should stand erect again and stretch one arm at a time as high as possible, alternating the arms. Then, he should drop over in the rag doll position and inhale while bent over. The body should be brought up very *easily,* retaining the breath that was inhaled while in the rag doll position. When the body is up, one should exhale, allowing the lower abdomen to come in and the chest cavity to remain high.

The last exercise for the torso is the ballet stretch described in Chapter 7.

Body Alignment

It is important to speak to a choir about what I refer to as body alignment. (Many people refer to it as "posture.")

In an effort to attain good body alignment, certain body landmarks should be noted. The singer should first place his hand just above the pubic bone; the other other hand should be at the end of the sternum.

The next thing to stress is that the tailbone should be pulled under (or rolled under, however one may wish to think of it). Doing this unlocks the knees (they are flexed—not bent or straight and tight). The tailbone being pulled under also rolls the pelvis under. This allows the lower part of the

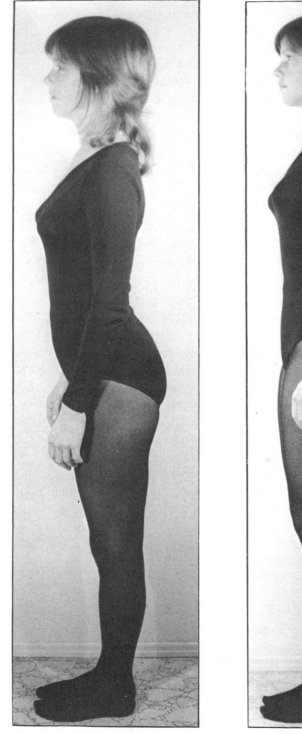

Figure 99
Body alignment—knees locked (incorrect)

Figure 100
Correct body alignment

abdomen to have an entirely different feeling than it does when the tailbone is out and the knees are locked. If the knees are locked or stiff, it pulls the whole pelvis in a different position and it pulls the lower part of the abdominal area in a different position and one is never able to have the flexibility in that area with the tailbone out that he would otherwise have.

Now with the body in correct alignment (Figures 99, 100), each choir member should stretch in the spine. The tailbone is under, the shoulders have been pulled back and down, the chest feels wide across the front. Everyone should now whisper "hook" (Chapter 6) three or four times, always allowing the lower abdominal area to pop out as the "k" is put on.

Inside Smile

Each choir member should be asked to close his mouth, but not his teeth, and smile as though he is smiling at someone in the room but does not wish the other person to see him smiling. This is what I call an "inside smile" (Figure 3). I have observed choirs whose directors have said to them, "Now smile— smile," and what they do is smile just on the outside—this is a grimace. In so doing, the choir gets a white tone; this will never allow a warm tone to come from those voices.

It is true that one feels something happening in the mask as he is doing this. He should feel the little muscles underneath the eyes being activated, but if he pulls up the muscles of his face (a grimace—Figure 4) and thinks nothing of the upward yawning feeling, these muscles will not lift the soft palate—and the soft palate is the very thing we wish to become activated and strong.

Vocal Exercises

First of the vocal exercises is the "hee-ah" (Figure 23); this will immediately start the breath being hooked into the tone. At first, singers should be allowed to sing it four or five times, gradually lengthening the number of times on one breath. They should then try singing it as long as possible, letting the abdomen come in gradually. They should be reminded, however, never to go so far in the exercise that the chest begins to drop. The chest should remain quiet or perhaps, if individual choir members are lucky when they begin, their chests will, as they should, begin to come up as they are singing. Some chests are so weak they do not even move. The main thing for choir members to remember is that their chests should not drop as they are singing this exercise. It should be taken up a half step at a time, perhaps three or four half steps, and then the choir should go on to the next exercise. Related to what I said earlier regarding having a "happy choir," I sometimes let my choirs run contests on the "hee-ah," seeing which member can go the longest—just for fun.

The "k" exercises should be given next to a choral group (Figures 24, 42, 43, and 44). The "k" automatically activates the soft palate, strengthening it and giving it more flexibility. Choir members should be cautioned never to sing back on the soft palate. We *always* think of singing the tone front. The "k" takes care of the back space in our soft palate area.

The next exercise is "flah-flah-nee" (Figure 25). The whole choir should begin in the middle range, C triad, in unison. The exercise should be sung up about four or five half steps and then back down.

The jaw and the tongue should *always* work together. I've seen some choir directors warming up their choirs, for instance, with a "lah-lah-lah-lah-lah" with the jaw held stiff and the tongue doing all the work. I know the director wants the tongue to be very loose but, to me, getting that looseness in this way is disastrous to the tone because, when the jaw is not allowed to move and the tongue is up against the upper front teeth, there is a pulling on the inside and outside of the throat at the root of the tongue. (If one places his fingers on his neck, where the tongue muscles come down into the neck, he will find that there is a slight tenseness when the jaw is down and the tongue is up. We want no tenseness in that area at all.) *The jaw and tongue should always work together*.

The singers should then put their hands on their waists and do a short snuff, just as though they are snuffing their noses, *very easily*. The lower abdominal area should spring out on the snuff. They should then sing the "snuff-zoh" (Figure 51).

The choir members should have impressed on them that the lower abdominal area must have that "snap-out" feeling in order to let the breath come into the lungs correctly and not be high up in the chest area. Figure 52 is then sung by the choir and then Figure 53 is sung with the choir feeling the rhythm very strongly.

The next exercise is the "zay-luh, zah-luh" (Figure 54). The choir should start in unison, letting the altos and basses drop out when necessary, but allowing the sopranos and tenors to go maybe two or three more half steps. The higher voices should then come back down and all join together in the middle range, dropping the sopranos and tenors out and letting the basses and altos go on down into the lower range. One can also let the low and high voices combine the exercise, doing it a third apart.

After the choir has sung Figure 54, they should then use the exercise for increasing the intensity of the tone (Figure 55). They should learn that the brain impulse will allow them to *think* the tone coming into the bones of the face on the forte tone. After the choir feels where that tone is vibrating, which is right in the bones up underneath the eyes and the nasal cavity, they will feel an intensity there as they are going into the crescendo on the top of the third.

Using this exercise will help a director explain an intense tone without causing the choir to *push* the tone. It is acquired simply by keeping the back spaces open and letting the tone "sit" in the "snuffing area" that is opened by the snuff in this exercise. The choir should also sing Figure 55 with a heady tone, again mentally directing the tone, or *letting* the tone go back up and over the soft palate without losing the focus of the tone.

GENERAL CHORAL COMMENTS

Naturally, I do not recommend that you do all of these exercises at any one rehearsal. I vary the exercises and they are scattered over many rehearsals. All choral directors are pressed by that clock which is hanging on the wall. *It is imperative, however, that warm-ups be done before any choral singing,* to insure that the choir members will not be straining their voices and so they will feel the breath and the tone going together.

The choir should start the exercises *lightly*—never full voice to start. Does an athlete jump up on the race track and start his 100-yard dash without warming up his legs? Does the pole vaulter try his highest jump to start with? Does a baseball player pitch his fastest ball to start with? No! Athletes all warm up those muscles gradually. Singing is parallel to athletics.

If the choir will be singing a piece, for instance, that needs a lot of big dynamic tones, I always use the "zay-luh, zah-luh" crescendo exercise (Figure 55). If they are going to sing something that is a capella, I will use a "zoh" where they sing it first letting the voice roll, and then the second time singing the scale through headily. I always include the "zay-luh, zah-luh" exercise (Figure 55) so that they can get the sensation of that tone resonating in the nasal cavity and in the oral cavity.

I stress that the tailbone must always be under, letting the body swing into the tone, letting the muscles of the legs feel as though they are flowing into the tone from the balls of the feet straight up into the lower abdominal area and on up into the thoracic cavity. I feel that the choir director also should stress that, as with all singers, the choir member should never give all the tone it is possible for him to give. When one gives the full amount of tone that one can, the tone is usually harsh. One should always be singing on the "interest" of the tone rather than the "principal." When some of the tone is reserved, that tone will be much more beautiful.

Along this line, if a singer is sitting between two voices that are larger than his, he should not begin to push his voice to make it large. This will also be a forced tone and never a beautiful one.

Some choirs must sing sitting in modern chairs which are bad for body alignment. The body alignment must be just the same seated as it is standing (Figure 101). The spinal column must be straight, the tailbone must be under, the shoulders must be down in the back. The neck is straight. If the choir happens to be sitting in what I call "bucket bottomed chairs," they should slip out to the edge of them. They cannot possibly sit in chairs that are hollowed out and get the body alignment right. They should sit on the edge of the chairs,

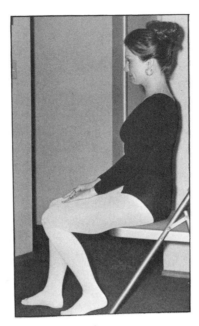

Figure 101
Correct sitting position for choral rehearsal

keeping their bodies in a straight alignment, their necks straight, with the head in a level position. The music should be held so they can see the choir director without pulling their chins up. (If the head and chin are pulled up, the vocal instrument is pulled out of position, and the column of air is changed, therefore changing the tone quality.)

It is very important that the director not leave his choir sitting or standing through a whole rehearsal. They should be allowed to alternate. If the choir seems to be getting a little bit fatigued, the director should stop and let them do the rag doll exercise and they will have new energy come into their bodies. How exciting it is to have a fine choral rehearsal. One is completely invigorated after such an experience.

Figure 102
Comfortable Ranges and Maximum Ranges for the Average Choir Member

A choral director should always know his group. Some years are peak years, others lean. It is dangerous, yes, harmful to choose music just because the conductor has always loved a particular selection and has hoped someday to conduct it. If it is *beyond* his choral group vocally, it should be left alone.

A *few* notes in the extreme ranges can often be effective (if you have the voices who can sing them easily). It should be remembered, however, that singers should not be forced to sing the pitches if they are out of reach at that particular time in the singer's development. Pieces which remain in comfortable limits of the voice will always be more beautiful in tone quality.

CONTESTS AND FESTIVALS

Choral festivals are important because they give students and directors the opportunity of hearing other choirs of comparable size. A director should never try to impress judges in festivals and contests by exploiting his singers. The choir should not sit listening to other choirs right up to the time of their own appearance. They must have at least fifteen minutes for their warm-ups before going on stage to sing. They must also have an adequate place for their warm-ups. This is *imperative*. The director should keep their talking down to a minimum before they perform.

The singers should be impressed with the idea that they are singing for the *joy* of singing—not that their lives depend upon a superior rating. They will be better performers with this in mind. If they enter the contest feeling that they are channels of joy, they will *give* joy and *get* joy.

MUSICAL THEATER

How important is this subject of musical theater to choir directors and drama departments! So many of our high schools and colleges (even some junior high schools) are producing Broadway shows. This is all well and good as long as those in charge of these young voices know what to expect and what not to expect from untrained voices. Voices at high school and college level are sometimes trained, but even then, most do not know how to get the "belting sound" in a way which will not injure their young voices. (See the discussion on belting in Chapter 11.)

I have heard junior high through high school level students in Broadway shows. One production of *Once Upon a Mattress* was done extremely well. Another show the following year in the same city, done with the same age group, was very badly done, really injuring the voices.

The first director was a drama major and had been a voice student of mine for five years. This group had done four performances of *Once Upon a Mattress,* the fourth being on a Saturday night after a matinee on that same day. I was truly thrilled to hear how fresh all these singers were at the end of the fourth performance! *Why* were they fresh? Because the director knew what she was doing with *both* the singing voice and the speaking voice.

In the dialogue, all of the lower abdominal area should be used for support (Chapter 6) and the wide snuff exercise (Figure 47) should also be used so that the speaking voice will not become fatigued. If a student has not been trained how to *speak* the dialogue "in character" *properly,* he will never be able to sing the solo well which follows it.

I heard a high school group playing *How to Succeed in Business Without Really Trying.* The leading man lost his voice the night before the opening! The same thing has happened in college level productions.

How can we prevent this from happening? *First* and most important, the director should choose music within the scope of his singers. If some of the music (say "Climb Every Mountain" from *The Sound of Music*) has too wide a range for the student to sing, it should be transposed (or the ending rewritten) so the song will be within the vocal reach of that young singer. Arias in opera are often transposed down or climactic spots rewritten for a particular singer. It is no disgrace. But it *is* a disgrace if the director has caused a voice to be ruined.

Second, the conductor must know vocal production. The same principles apply to both singing and speaking: breath support, spaces open in the throat and the soft palate area, and correct use of the lips, tongue and mask. All these techniques are dealt with in detail in this book.

Third, one should not try to choreograph a number until the students know their music *completely.* Even after they do know the music, they should not be permitted to sing it while learning the routine of the number. Much harm can be done to the voice if allowing the student to sing while learning the dance routine.

A SPECIAL NOTE TO CHOIR DIRECTORS

You have a great deal to do with how your group is going to sing. Develop a sense of humor. Good discipline is also imperative, but I feel there should always be periods in a rehearsal of "letting down." Too rigid a discipline through a complete rehearsal does not allow for that. One should keep in mind, however, that no talking should be allowed by the other sections while one section is working specifically on a "trouble spot."

How your choir sings is influenced by the use of your hands! A sudden downbeat of the hand and arm for an attack can cause the choir to "pound" the first pitch of the phrase. Likewise, when the director wants a pianissimo, if he "shushes" the choir with a sudden "sh!" it will cause members of the group to grab the tone in their throats to close it off, rather than allowing it to go up into a "heady tone." As you probably know, the correct signal can be given very gently just by turning the palm of the hand toward the choir. The dynamic crescendo or attack can be done with a good definite cue beat, but not a banged or muscular one. Energy must flow from the director to his group, and the expression of his face (a reflection of that inside smile of which I have spoken so much) can help the choir make a joyful sound.

Let me stress again that you should get the music into their minds, ears, and tongues before you let them try to sing it. Much harm is done by trying to do "everything at once." If a piece is a rapid number, sing it slowly until all the above is accomplished (music in ear, rhythm in ear, text in tongue). Study the music carefully before attempting to direct it. Allow your choir members to take home their music and work on their parts as though they were soloists, contributing the best vocalism at all times. Do not allow your singers to press on the low tones, and do not allow them to push on the top range.

Keep energy in your "piano" dynamic so that it will be alive and intense and will be supported.

We all want a beautiful sound to come from our groups. I feel that sound *comes* when the principles of this technique are applied. The voices will always blend, they will always be "under control." When the consonants are precise and rhythmic, one will have good articulation. When the vowels are well formed, well focused, and maintain their shape throughout the range and dynamic levels, one will have a beautiful tone quality.

During the Baroque period, when music was sometimes written for boys' choirs, there was one quality or "choral sound" prevalent. I have often heard choral directors, directing adults singing Baroque music, ask them to take the vibrato out of their voices. The beautiful boy soprano voice has a *natural* vibrato in it. (It will not sound like the female soprano, but neither is it a straight sound.) Only by using boy sopranos can one achieve a boy soprano sound which is not a *straight white* tone. No singer should be asked to copy the sound of another singer; this can be disastrous to any voice.

SINGING ON MIKES

Today we see and hear many choral groups on television. We see them singing through "mikes." If there are no hand mikes, a director should always be careful in the "line-up" of the choir. I have observed a 6' 3" boy singing with a girl who is probably 4' 6" on one mike. The young man cannot possibly keep his body in alignment and sing into the mike; therefore, his throat is going to suffer for it. *Guard* your singers. If a hand mike is held, the singer should be sure to keep his chest wide—he should never let his arm pull the mike in and allow the chest to sink. The voice will ''pay the toll'' sooner or later.

THE IMPORTANCE OF CHURCH ORGANISTS

How grateful we all should be for fine church organists. It is important, however, that the choral director be very aware of the balance between his choir and the organ. How often have I heard an organist completely cover the beautiful singing of the choir. The only way for a choir director to be certain that this is not happening is to stand back in the area where the congregation is seated so he can *hear* the balance.

I love a big organ sound, if the introduction to the anthem calls for it, but organists should be careful to give only a ''supporting'' accompaniment when the choir sings. During the congregational singing, the organist can really guide the congregation by his leadership under the singing. To me it is unforgivable for an organist to suddenly drop the support out from under that glorious congregational singing. Martin Luther had congregational rehearsals for the hymns which were to be sung on Sunday. Wouldn't it be good if we could in some way have more congregational participation? There is nothing more moving than great congregational singing for any church service, but the congregation can sing only what it knows.

Whatever we do in our wonderful support by the choir in our church services, we should remember that one of the world's greatest composers of choral music, Johann Sebastian Bach, wrote at the top of each composition, ''All for the Glory of God,'' and we should make our contribution as choral directors as great as it can be.

KEY POINTS TO REMEMBER

1. Choral warm-ups are imperative.
2. A choral director should remind his group of the necessity for correct body alignment, breath support, the use of the inside smile, and other facets of correct singing technique.
3. A choir should be careful of body alignment when singing while seated.
4. All music chosen must be written within the vocal and dramatic reach of the cast or choir being worked with at that particular time.
5. In musical theater, correct *speaking* principles must be taught as well as correct *singing* technique.

6. Choir directors should always consider how their hands and faces reflect the sound they want from their group. They must guard against the choir grabbing sudden piano passages in their throats or pushing for forte sections.

7. A singer using a microphone must keep in mind the importance of keeping good body alignment.

13

HOW TO DEAL WITH PROBLEMS OF THE THROAT:

CASE STUDIES AND EXERCISES

In this chapter, I will deal with the problems of rebuilding a voice after it has been affected by such things as polyps and nodules on the vocal cords, hemorrhaging of the cords, laryngitis, and psychological trauma and what to do after a tonsillectomy.

> For a stated period of time specific vocal exercises must be given for the individual case, to correct the condition and followed by a period of rest. One case may require stronger palate action, another, positive exercising of the ventricular and base of tongue regions, in order to regain balance of laryngeal pulling and perfect cord stretching.[1]

There is nothing more gratifying to a teacher of voice than to enable an artist who is having serious vocal problems to regain complete vocal facility and to continue with a career. I suppose the reason that I have become so interested in this particular area is because of my own experience which I related in the early part of this book.

About six years ago, a woman who was a very fine teacher and who had been a fine singer came to me for help. When she first sang for me it was as though she was singing through a veil. I immediately asked if she had seen a laryngologist. She said she had and was told that her cords were in fine condition. I immediately began working with the therapeutic exercises as found in Chapter 8, but the voice did not respond.

During her third lesson, as she began to sing, two pitches sounded at once. I knew then that something was pathologically wrong and I sent her to my own laryngologist. While examining her throat, he found a polyp under her right vocal cord. He said that it had to be removed immediately as it could be

---
[1]Frank E. Miller, *Vocal Art Science* (New York, G. Schirmer, Inc., 1922).

cancerous. He felt that the polyp had been caused by singing a role in an opera production which was not correct for her vocally. It was possible that a blood vessel had broken, causing the polyp to form.

Following her surgery, I invited her to stay in my home where I could watch her very carefully during her recuperation. On the second day after surgery she began speaking, but only a little, and very easily. A week following the surgery her surgeon told her that she could begin to vocalize five minutes a day.

As quickly as I was able to start her vocalizing, I began again with the therapeutic exercises (Chapter 8). It was like watching a butterfly come out of a cocoon. The voice quality was clear and a beautiful warm tone started to come forth. This singer is now performing in Europe as well as America and is one of our very fine teachers here in this country.

EACH VOCAL PROBLEM IS UNIQUE

There is no set formula for beginning therapeutic exercise. It is imperative that the teacher listen carefully to the sound being emitted from the student, and analyze what is wrong with that sound.

When the teacher starts with a node problem, he should start with therapeutic exercises. If the nodes have been caused by over-singing, or singing material which is not right for the voice, the student should, if possible, discontinue singing for a brief time, perhaps two weeks. If he is in a performance and "the show must go on" he should still begin the exercises and bring in the literature he is performing so the teacher can discover the cause for his problems.

Speakers acquire nodes as often as do singers. When one does not speak correctly it is practically impossible to sing well. How does one speak correctly? He should carry over the same principles used for singing: breath support, wide spaces in nasopharynx and oral cavities, and loose jaw.

GENERAL CAUSES OF VOCAL PROBLEMS

Incorrect body alignment (posture) (Figures 99 and 100)

Lack of breath support

Tight jaw

. Incorrect tongue positions

In my years of experience, laryngologists have sent me patients who have had hemorrhaging vocal cords, patients with a history of laryngitis for two years (with final loss of the voice), patients who have nothing but a squeak coming out when they try to speak, and patients with nodes on the cords. It is imperative that each patient learn good body alignment first.

The patient who came with hemorrhaging of the cords was a lecturer in demand all over the United States. He had been taught to pull in the abdomen very tightly and to keep the chest high. This was absolutely the opposite of what he should have been doing. He also was clearing his throat constantly; this was the first thing I told him he must abstain from doing. The feeling of a need to clear the throat was caused by an uncomfortable feeling there, but by clearing it, he was forcing the cords to be pulled into an abnormal position. (If one feels the necessity to clear the throat, and the cause comes from mucus on the cords, one should use a very light puff of air coming by the lower abdomen pulling in as in an *easy* cough forcing air through the cords to push the mucus away. He should swallow, and if the mucus feels like it is still there, he should leave it alone. It will gradually remove itself by correct use of the voice.) The need to clear the throat can also be caused by nerves or simply from *habit*.

The patient who came to me with a history of laryngitis for over two years and had completely lost her voice—no sound whatsoever was coming out of her throat—was in politics, speaking constantly. She had a sunken chest and round shoulders. She also drank a great deal of alcohol and smoked constantly. I put her on complete vocal rest for two weeks, insisting that she *write* everything that she wished to communicate. She was not even allowed to whisper. (Whispering can be even more damaging than speaking.) I also told her she should stop smoking completely, if possible, and refrain from the use of alcohol.

I worked with these people for three half-hour sessions per week for a period of less than three months. They both left the studio with their speaking voices in good order.

Two other patients came to me with nothing but squeaks coming out. One had been a professional singer and was a college voice teacher. After surgical removal of nodes, she was not able to utter a sound of any kind for one whole year. She had been to speech therapists and laryngologists and no one seemed to understand why she could not speak. This patient worked with me twice a week for thirty minutes at a time, and continued in her college position, teaching music. At the end of six months, she was not only speaking but beginning to sing with a beautiful quality. She has been continuing her work with me for about a year. Her speaking voice is quite normal and her singing voice is continuing to grow.

The other patient had been an elementary school teacher and had lost her voice and then her teaching position. She has been studying with me for two months. She had a lot of speech therapy and psychiatric help before coming to me.

With these two patients sharing the *same* symptoms (a squeak for a voice, almost impossible to understand), I nevertheless found that I had to approach them each *differently*.

TWO CASE HISTORIES

Following are the details of the work each of these women has done with me. It is my hope that the procedures outlined here will give other teachers some idea of how to approach similar problems, always remembering that each case must be dealt with individually.

I found that the woman who had been a singer had very fine posture as far as the torso and the rest of the body alignment was concerned; however the tone would simply not come from her throat. There was no phonation except squeaks.

The first thing I had her do was to blow her breath out by pulling the abdomen in and then let the abdomen spring out, allowing the breath to come into the lungs. Then I had her get her shoulder blades touching in back, pulling them back, then letting the shoulders come forward (but not any farther than where the chest would *remain straight across*.) I had her do this very gently, being careful not to lift the shoulders but simply to pull the shoulders straight back. On the fourth time, I had her pull the shoulder blades down in the back. Finding this position is so important since the chest is one of the most important areas for the speaking voice. It must be wide and strong.

The next thing I had her do was to smile naturally. As she had the smile on her face I asked her to keep those mask muscles involved and swing the jaw down three or four times.

The next exercise was the rag doll exercise (Chapter 7), making sure that her chest stayed wide when coming back to the standing position. With some students this is impossible at first because this area is weak. (That is certainly one of the reasons that this particular patient was having trouble with her speaking voice.)

The next exercise this former singer did was the wide snuff (Figure 47). One of the reasons that a person has difficulty with his throat in singing or speaking is that all the musculature of the vocal mechanism, the jaw, or the soft palate, is tense, completely restricting tone. This wide snuff is one of the finest exercises that I know to help get that throat area wide and open, ready for the tones to pass through it.

I had her do the "hook" exercise (Chapter 6), then the wide snuff, combining the supporting part of the abdominal area which she had felt on the "hook" and the musculature of the face from the wide snuff. Then I had her speak "fah-ee-ah-ee-ah." The tone was not clear. I watched very closely what was happening and noticed that her jaw was shooting out as she would say the "fah." (Doing this would pull muscles in the throat and automatically cause it not to be as open as it should be.) So I asked her to simply go through the motions (but without speaking) of saying "fah-ee-ah." Then we went back to the "hook" and wide snuff, and then, thinking of a straight-down jaw, she said "fah-ee-ah-ee-ah."

The next exercise was "mah." She did the wide snuff again, and said "mah-mah-mah," always feeling support from the hook muscle. With the "mah-mah-mah" there is the feeling of a smile on the inside which lifts the outside mask (the inside smile). This was the end of the first lesson. These therapeutic lessons are very concentrated, and one should not schedule them to last longer than thirty minutes.

On the second lesson, I had her start again with the "hook," then the wide snuff, and then feel a slight resistance at the lower part of the abdominal area as she said "fah-ee-ah, fee-ah-ee" and then "mah-mah-mah." (Remember, this patient had been a very fine singer so I could start her thinking about a *resistance* at the lower abdomen. This is not a tight feeling, but the abdomen must not go way in on the first word that is said.) The next exercise I gave her was "hee-oh," always thinking of the inside smile. In the third lesson I included the circle arm breath (Figures 37, 38, 39, 40).

One of the most important reasons for people having vocal problems, be they speakers or singers, is incorrect breath support. This is why I use the "hook" exercises as much as I do—to help build the strength of the chest and lower abdomen—and why I use the circle arm breath to help build the whole thoracic cavity. When one first starts using the "hook" exercise the chest simply may not move. It is as though it were dead, but as the student continues to use the "hook" exercise, he will find more strength coming into his lower abdominal area to help with the breath support, and he will also find that there is much more strength coming into the chest area.

Another cause of vocal problems is the back of the tongue. Even though one may not see pressure there (sometimes one can see it very plainly) the tongue muscles can be tight. The exercise that helps eliminate this problem is the "ng-ah" (Chapter 8). Again, the mask is wide and the jaw is dropped at the hinge.

I asked this particular student to do the "ng-ah" only when she was with me and not to try to do it at home alone. I asked her also not to make any sound, but simply to work the musculature of the correct mask muscles, jaw hinge muscles, and the back of the tongue muscles. (This exercise should never be repeated more than three times.)

Again, in this lesson we returned to the wide snuff and used "kee-kay-kee." The "k" grabbed in the throat, so I stopped that exercise immediately because I knew that something was wrong with the soft palate area or else the "k" would come very easily. Later we came back to it.

We then worked with the frontal consonant "d" speaking "day" and "dah." We went back to the "ng-ah" *without any sound* again. We did a wide snuff and said "joice." Then "lah-lah-lah," *the jaw and the tongue moving together* on the "l," and "loh-loh-loh," the jaw and tongue still moving together. We were then able, in about the fourth or fifth lesson (always review-ing what we had done in the previous lesson), to say "take." Then I had her say "I told you so." When she started a sentence with a vowel, there was always a glottal attack. One could hear a little pop on the cords. I would have her do a wide snuff completely, then just the first half of the wide snuff, and as she started to say "I," swing the jaw; there was no glottal attack because the breath was underneath the tone, the vocal cords were in correct position, and they phonated in perfect sound.

Gradually as we worked week after week, the throat began to be open and the sound was beginning to be normal. I then started the "preh" exercise (Figure 33) with her (only the musculature, not the actual sound). As when sung, the speaking voice sits in the teeth on this exercise. One feels the speaking voice against the hard palate and strength in the upper lip.

I never speak of pitch levels, instead letting the student think of simply putting the breath support underneath the tone, keeping the throat open, and speaking on whatever pitch he is comfortable with at that time. Sometimes it is very high, but I never say "lower the pitch," since when one uses this expres-sion, a person many times presses down on the larynx to get the sound he wants.

I have also had the experience of singers and patients coming to me who have been told they are speaking too low. They try to lift the pitch and in so doing they pull up the whole mechanism of the throat and it just becomes tighter.

A voice will find the level where it is easy to speak. It will have resonance in it. It will also have carrying power and control when the breath support is right, the chest is strong and not collapsing, and the resonating spaces are open (from the wide snuff), the back tongue muscles are loose (from the "ng-ah" exercise) and the nasal cavity is open (from the "preh"). When all of this musculature is correct, and it will become correct through these exercises, there will be a resonant beautiful sound in the voice.

The next exercise we worked with was "lah-bay-dah-may-nee-poh-too," still remembering the space in the throat, the wide chest, and the breath sup-port. We say three syllables at a time on one breath until the student has breath support to say all seven on one breath. I had the patient do a "hook" between each group of three. The "lah-bay-dah-may-nee-poh-too" exercise is one that starts combining vowels and consonants in a sentence-like structure. We then said "mah-may-mee-moh-moo," feeling much strength in the mask on the "m." If the throat began to grab at any one spot, I had her stop and do the "hook," a complete wide snuff, and then the first half of one, speaking on the breath obtained on the first half, and the throat functioned beautifully. It was when the breath support went out from underneath her that the throat muscles began to close in and restrict the tone grabbing in her throat.

Up to now we had not even tried to sing at all. I should say we did try to sing in about the second lesson, but the sound was dreadful, so we stayed away from any sung sound until about the second month. Remember, she was still teaching, handling her choirs and teaching voice. Ordinarily I would not have allowed her to have spoken at all when beginning these exercises, but she had a position and her administration was kind enough to allow her to continue in her work at the school. She was an excellent musician with a very keen mind, so she was able to continue teaching and gradually regain her speaking voice.

When I felt that the speaking voice was far enough along, I asked her to sing a skip of a third, 5 to 3, on "fah-ee," *not holding the last tone*. I reminded her to keep the same feeling as she had had when speaking the exercises: breath support underneath, spaces open in the throat, the wide snuff and inside smile positions, and allowing the jaw to swing straight down. She did the wide snuff and then sang "fah-ee." Then she sang "fee-ah." I was quite pleased that there was a singing tone there ready to start to work with.

The "k," which was impossible to use earlier in our work together, now came very easily. We used it on "kee-kah," then "kah-kee." This was a singing tone on *one pitch*. It was staccato. The next exercise she sang was "thee-ah" (5 — 3) and "thah-ee" (unvoiced "th"). We went up about four or five half steps. As we worked, I kept reminding her of the strength in the upper lip which she had gained from the "preh" exercise and to feel the tone coming front, keeping the back spaces open—the same feeling she had had from the wide snuff exercise. Then we went to the "nah-ee," reminding her of the "n" feeling very wide across the mask. I would stop her many times and have her do a "hook" so she would not be short of breath at any time.

Many times the "oo" is difficult for singers. I discovered in working with this student that the "oo" was one of the easiest vowels for her, so we started on the 5-4-3-2 with "boo" and ending on "ah" on 1. It was easier for her to start c″, each first tone going up to the f or f sharp above that. We kept it in a very short range at first, gradually letting the final vowel "boo-ee" or "boo-ah" come into the lower part of the voice.

She told me that when she had the node on the cords she had sung a raw chest tone down in the low range. It was interesting as I worked with her to find that this low range (from g′ down to c′) was the last part of the voice that came in easily.

We gradually began working on the exercise of rolling the tongue forward, the top of the tongue behind the front teeth, the mask very wide on "nee" (Chapter 8) *only* on 3-2-1. Then we did the same thing with "nah" on 3-2-1, never holding the last pitch. Then we did the "fee-ah" on 5-3-1 and we went up to f′. We were finally able to get down to the c′.

It was not more than three or four lessons later when she came in and said, "I feel better speaking now after I have been singing." This pleased me to no end because I knew that the singing voice was on a higher line inside and she would have less trouble then with her speaking voice. The speaking and the singing voice are very closely related. When one speaks incorrectly, one will never be able to sing as well; therefore, we had to get her speaking voice to the point where it could function before she could sing.

We found that the "thee-ah" skip of a third from 3 — 1 was easier for her at first than "thah-ee" on the same figure, so gradually we worked until the "ee" would come in. It did not happen for three or four more lessons. The "boo" was really the easier for her, and we were finally able to take the entire octave clear up to an f″. The "ah" was beginning to come. Then we used an "n" (which brings the vowel forward) on "nee-ah" and it seemed to be even more helpful than the "thee-ah." She had the back spaces open now, the tongue was free in the back, the soft palate was free and therefore we could work with the "nee-ah" with much more ease.

We then worked the "hum-ee," the "h" being an aspirant and the "m" feeling very full and wide under the eyes. We gradually went to the skip of 5-3-1, "thee-oh-ah," feeling an arch on the inside of the oral cavity all the way down. In her case, we began on the octave above c′ almost continuously; at first that was where the voice seemed to be the most free. During all of this, I had her do the rag doll drop and the wide snuff *many times.*

Finally I had her start with the "lah-bay-dah-may-nee," this time singing it on 5-4-3-2-1, taking a breath, going up a half step, inside smile, the hook muscle working, and in two weeks she was doing the entire octave.

At this point, I began letting her try some of the early Italian classics, applying the principles of the technique with which we had been working. I was delighted to hear her sing these songs with a good quality in the voice. This took place very gradually and her voice was never forced.

After this, we began working on the "ng" exercise (Figure 29) and were able to get the "ng" on 5-3-1, staccato, letting the jaw swing on each pitch. We were able to get it down to c′. I used a great deal of the shoulder stretching exercise on her as we worked through this whole period.

This has been one of the most gratifying experiences of all my years of teaching. I shall never forget the first day when everything began to coordinate and she spoke with a normal tone. Tears streamed down her face as she left the studio. A week or two passed by and she said, "It is such a joy to be able to speak and not have people turn around and look at me wondering what is wrong—why I cannot speak with a normal sound like everyone else. If my singing voice comes back, this will only just be bonus. I'm so thrilled with what is happening to my speaking voice!" I, too, have been very gratified and rewarded, for the sound of the singing voice is also coming along now as she is continuing with the study of voice.

The next patient to be discussed is a woman who came to me only able to squeak as she tried to speak. She had been a teacher in the lower grades. She told me that she had lost her voice gradually, over a period of three years. It had become so bad that she had to take a leave of absence from her school position. She had gone to a psychiatrist as well as a speech therapist, trying to get help. It was the psychiatrist who sent her to me; he felt that much of her trouble had been caused by an emotional situation. But, as he is a fine singer himself, he also said, "I feel there is more there than just the emotional side. I feel a great deal of it is probably functional. Will you try to see if you can help her?"

When I started with her I did get a little history of what had caused the voice to deteriorate. And it was true, there had been a great deal of emotional stress. The vocal instrument itself is a very sensitive instrument. When one is depressed or under stress one feels it in the throat almost more quickly than in the rest of the body. I hope the reader remembers my story of personal stress that I mentioned in Chapter 8. I *do* know that emotions have a great deal to do with the voice. One can always tell when a person is sad, glad, weak, or excited, by the sound that comes out of that person.

The psychiatrist had been very helpful in finding out the reasons for her anxiety and had helped her a great deal in this area. I simply told her that I knew this emotional stress certainly would not help the voice, and it could have helped bring on the condition in which she found herself. She seemed to be in better spirits having understood herself better than she had before going to the psychiatrist, so I began there and went on with her in the therapeutic work.

She had only fair posture; she was not what I would call a round shouldered person, but she did not stand with correct body alignment. The first thing we worked on was to get the body in alignment; I gave her many body building exercises, just as I had given the first patient.

I also asked her not to speak aloud for one week, but to write everything that she wished to say. I told her that as long as she tried to speak outside of the lesson, until we got the voice functioning correctly, she would only slow down the process. She was willing to do this. I also told her I did not want her to do any whispering. Her assignment was to see me in the first week for three thirty minute sessions—and no talking of any kind.

She was a very cooperative patient. After getting the body alignment started in the right direction, we started to work with the mask. It was literally impossible to get her to lift her cheek muscles at all. Only when she began to really laugh did the muscles start to come up under the eyes. I said, "Let the jaw swing from that width you feel under the eyes." When she tried to do this consciously at first, it was very difficult. I had her use a mirror to see what she was trying to do. We had to work about three weeks before she was able to do even this.

She was not as muscularly coordinated as the other patient because she had never been a singer, but we worked very hard with the chest area, with the pulling back of the shoulders. This shoulder stretching would always come after the "hook" and the circle arm breath. I had her do the rag doll drop a number of times in the lesson. I had her then mouth—without sound—"mah-mee-dah-dee." Her tongue was pulling back very badly in her mouth. I had her again think of the "smile width" under the eyes and drop the jaw loosely in the back. (The jaw hinge so often is a problem with the speaking or singing voice. People speak with their jaws very tight. This constricts the vocal sound because it constricts the whole instrument.) I had her physically exercise her mask muscles and the dropping of the jaw, leaving the tongue to the front. It did not want to stay in the front at all at first. She had to watch a mirror and go at it very consciously, even mechanically at first.

She was very weak in the lower abdominal area so I gave her the "sh-sh-sh" exercise (Figure 56) allowing the abdomen to come in very slowly and letting the chest area widen. On the fourth lesson we started on the wide snuff. When I looked into her mouth, it was impossible to see the soft palate because the tongue was so bunched. I knew, therefore, that we had to do a little bit of therapy with the tongue. I gave her the "ng-ah" exercise (Chapter 8) but again not making any sound. *No sound was allowed out of the throat* because the voice would add problems by tying up the throat. We used the exercises without sound to "massage" her throat. On the "mah-dah" I insisted that she just barely touch the tone, barely speak, keeping the mask wide and letting the jaw swing loosely, no tone coming out.

On the fifth lesson I still felt she was not getting all of her rib cage working, even on the circle arm breath exercise which I had given her two lessons previously, so we added the ballet stretch (Chapter 7).

On the seventh lesson we started with the wide snuff, wide mask, whispering the "hook," feeling the space, and saying "nah-dah-lah." The tone was beginning to come out of the throat without catching. (Previously the tone would start and suddenly stop and then begin again and stop.) The next lesson we started "mah-may-may" and then "lah-bay-dah," stopping for a "hook," and then "may-nee-poh."

After this lesson, I had her use the muscles as if she were saying "ming," feeling a lot of pull-up under the eyes, but I did not allow any sound on this exercise. It was simply to get the muscles involved and to think where that tone was going to sit when she said "ming." It was an exercise of the muscles of the face, and the feeling, and the thought. At this lesson, when she started speaking the "mah-dah-lah," the pitch was very high. I had already told her not to think about pitch level, but just to let the tone come where it would, and as she spoke her voice was almost like a child's voice.

When one is speaking, one should speak into the teeth with a feeling of great strength from the sternum underneath for the support of the tone. We therefore then began working on the "preh" (Figure 33) *without* any sound, simply moving the upper lip; I had her do this a number of times, and, after she had done it for about a two-week period, I asked her to say "lah-bay-dah-may-nee-poh-too," concentrating on the strength of the upper lip, and *the pitch came down into the teeth area*. I again assured her that when the support is there and the spaces are open and the musculature of the face (including the upper lip and the mask) is all coordinated, the pitch would come down to a level she would enjoy using. This is exactly what happened.

At the beginning of her sixth lesson, she wrote on her card to me (I still was not allowing her to speak outside of the exercises in the lesson), "When I'm working by myself I actually find myself expecting my voice to be bad and fear comes into me to speak. But when I practice my mask, mouth positions, the little snuff, and the circle arm—getting it all coordinated—then I can speak and nothing catches in my throat."

I said, "You cannot have faith and fear at the same time. When you fear something, you always block it. You have just said to me when you have gone through the mechanics of the exercises and then speak, the tone comes out with a good sound. Therefore, keep your faith in the exercises and that will push the fear thoughts out of your mind." This lesson came at the end of the second week (remember, I was seeing her three times a week), and for the first time she had a normal healthy tone.

At the beginning of the third week we started, as at all lessons, with a "hook," circle arm, shoulder stretch, the wide snuff (which she was able to do well with the tongue normal), and "ng-ah" without any sound yet. Then I started with a "hum" on one pitch, any pitch that came into her ear. This was the first time I had tried any kind of a singing tone with her.

At the next lesson, she asked if I would like to hear a tape which she had made during her practice. She was *singing* a little nursery rhyme and it was very interesting to hear how easily it was going. She said to me afterwards that it was easier for her to speak after she sang. You will remember the same thing happened with the other patient. After the speaking voice developed so that it would not grab in her throat, she started singing and she also said it was easier to speak after singing. Again it proved to me how close together are the functioning of the singing and speaking voices. From then on we worked with singing, then with speaking.

I had to be away about two and one-half weeks and was very eager to hear what progress she had made in my absence. She was able to speak with a normal tone. She still had to think very consciously of the wide ribs, chest, and mask, and the back throat being open, but, when they were, the speaking voice was normal. She has to go very slowly yet, and not as automatically as I know she will soon, because I am only seeing her once a week now. She is continuing singing the little kindergarten songs, very lightly, and the pitches are very accurate. When she was having the problems with her speaking voice she told me it was impossible to sing on pitch. The pitch problem has disappeared.

BASIC STEPS

The basic foundation for any voice rebuilding must start *first* with correct body alignment, which is imperative for correct breath support. The inside smile is the next thing one must think about. It is vital that the mask, the tongue, and the jaw be in correct coordination.

1. The first exercise usually used is *"fah-ee-ah."* The student should stop and do the "hook" before every one of these exercises is spoken so that the lower abdominal area is involved immediately and the lungs will fill with air, the chest (not shoulders) being high and straight across. The final "ah" should not be sustained. This exercise should be done once or twice, depending on the individual. The jaw should be swinging loosely from the hinge, with a wide mask under the eyes. The same exercise should then be done on *"fee-ah-ee."*

2. *Mah:* Wide mask; should not be sustained.

3. *Wide snuff:* Description in Chapter 8.

4. *Ng-ah:* Description in Chapter 9—to be spoken, not sung.

5. *Lah-bay-dah-may-nee-poh-too.* Taken one syllable at a time with the abdomen springing out between each syllable and the mask remaining wide because of the inside smile. Then three syllables should be spoken at a time, stopping to take a breath between each three, until all can be sustained on one breath with spaces open in the throat and with a strong mask.

When working with these problems, the teacher should be as positive in his approach as possible, bringing in humor to relieve tension. He should get his student smiling or laughing easily so that the mask is up and the throat open. Another pointer: if one consonant does not allow the vowel that follows to come easily, the teacher should not keep trying the same consonant. Instead, change it, always following the principles regarding vowels and consonants that are described in Chapter 9.

DEALING WITH SURGERY

For all of us, surgery is "bad news." Scientific progress, however, has made such strides in the past few years that I no longer have the fear I once had. I will not write of bad conditions which have come from surgery in the past, but I still feel that specific precautions should be taken for singers.

An anesthesiologist should *always* be told that his patient is a singer. During a general anesthetic, a tracheal tube must be passed through the vocal cords. A good anesthesiologist will be careful to see that this tube is the correct size, not too large or too small, and that care is taken as it passes through the cords so as not to cause an abrasion.

If the surgery is to be abdominal, the surgeon should be made aware of the potential problems of such surgery for a singer. He should then take all the care possible with the abdominal muscles so they will not have any undue scar tissue form; that would inhibit the elasticity of the abdominal muscles which are so important for breath control.

One should not try to sing too soon after any major surgery. A general anesthetic is always a great shock to the body. A singer must give the body time to recover and gain its strength before trying to sing up to his level before surgery.

WHAT TO DO AFTER A TONSILLECTOMY

A tonsillectomy should be done only when the tonsils are so diseased that they are making the body ill, or so enlarged that they are pulling down heavily on the soft palate and closing the opening to the throat to a very marked extent. If this is the case, one should go to the finest laryngologist he can find and have them out. A tonsillectomy *is not* a minor operation and a singer must know what to ask for.

One of my students, who was a finalist in the Metropolitan Opera Auditions, Western Division, and also one of six finalists at the national competition of the National Association of Teachers of Singing, had to have a tonsillectomy. She came through with "flying colors." We followed directions very specifically from her fine laryngologist: Wait until ten days after the surgery before there is any vocalizing, then, only five minutes a day, increasing to ten minutes a day. He explained that this is to keep adhesions from forming, and not running any risk of starting hemorrhaging before complete healing takes place.

After about two weeks she had her first lesson—thirty minutes only. The sound which came forth was a good, healthy sound. The voice was moving easily. She vocalized on the "ng" (Figure 31) up to b″. This pitch was in her normal range. When she began singing, we worked only on early Italian classics. We had a lesson the following day, and the voice went up to c#′″ on the "ng."

At the third lesson, three days later, she sang the arpeggio (Figure 66a) to c′″ but there was a tickle which started in the throat. This was a signal to me to go no further. When one has not used a muscle anywhere in the body (say in the case of a broken arm, when the arm is taken out of the cast for the first time), there is a slight tingling as the circulation begins to flow more normally. So it is with the throat. When a singer has not been vocalizing for a period of time and he begins to go up into the upper range, his throat will tingle or tickle a bit until the musculature is completely coordinated. He should always stop and wait until a period of hours has passed, then resume practicing—but not going to the top of his range that day.

Other than the "ng", the exercises which we first used were *all* triad exercises (nothing stepwise): "fah-ee-ah" (5-3-1), "fee-ah-ee" (5-3-1), "kee-kah-kee" (5-3-1), and "flah-flah-nee-ah-ee" (1-3-5-3-1). Her voice did not need to be "rebuilt," but careful use of the musculature was important. In her second lesson we used only five-tone scales *descending*.

A month from the day of surgery, this student was singing Rossini's "Una voce poca fa." The tone seemed even fuller than it had before her tonsils were taken out. (This does not mean that I am now advocating tonsillectomies, but I *am* grateful for a fine surgeon.) The "head voice" did not completely return until the soft palate area was once again flexible. The surgeon told us that the inflexibility was caused by the scar tissue which remains after any surgery. This was gradually worked out by the "k" exercises and the wide snuff.

She was able to sing only forty-five minutes at a time her first five lessons because her body had not yet recovered. She was told not to do her physical exercise program—in her case, bicycling—until three weeks after surgery. Until the tissue is completely healed, hemorrhaging can occur. (We were told that bleeding is rare and almost never occurs after the seventh day.) By her fifth lesson, her rib cage was still not as strong as before. We therefore waited until the body had its full strength back before starting any high dramatic sustained arias. The body *must* be strong before one attempts any dramatic singing. From the fifth lesson on she was able to sing the full hour.

Time is of great importance after any surgery. One's body must be strong or one will begin to feel the throat working—something we do not want. Nothing should ever be felt in the throat. A singer should not jump into big dramatic arias until his body is strong enough to support the breath, and then the vocal instrument will always function at its best.

KEY POINTS TO REMEMBER

1. An anesthesiologist must always be told his patient is a singer.
2. A surgeon should be made aware of the importance of the abdominal area to a singer if that is the area upon which surgery will be performed.
3. One should never try to sing too soon or too heavily after major surgery.
4. During recovery, one should start singing in short periods, gradually increasing the time as strength permits.

14

KEY QUESTIONS ON THIS TECHNIQUE
—WITH ANSWERS

The following are questions which have been asked frequently during my teaching career, both in my studio and in seminars. They deal with many of the key points covered in this book.

Will you explain the balanced tone?

It is a tone which uses the front pull-ups and the back pull-ups at the same time. (See Appendix 2.)

Why can you elide words in French songs and not in English?

Elision is a characteristic of the French language but not of the English language.

What do you do if only one side of your upper lip can be pulled up?

Start mentally, then *physically,* pulling up the side that does not lift.

Could you tell more about where pull-up muscles are and when to use them?

The back pull-up muscles are in the soft palate area, and the front pull-up muscles are in the nose and the mask muscles of the face. All of them are used for different effects. (See Chapter 11.)

What do you mean by the term "neutral vowel?"

One which is scarcely sounded when we speak it, such as in the last syllable of "evil." (See Chapter 9.)

What is your feeling about anaptyxis at the end of a word in order to emphasize the terminal consonant?

I do not like the end of a word to have an anaptyxis. In a final "d," for instance, there should be no sound past the placing of the "d" at the end of a word—no "did-uh."

I noticed in one of the "Met" winners a certain "tinny" quality—not unpleasant, but I was aware of it. Would this be the result of the arrangement of the larynx, etc., and/or could this be corrected to result in a rounder, more opulent tone?

The sound of a voice always becomes more beautiful with correct use. Sound of the voice depends upon resonator spaces; throat; chest cavity; laryngeal area; and size of vocal cords (length and thickness). The tinny quality is caused by lack of coordination of *all* of the above mentioned spaces.

How long do you keep students within a limited range or on the beginning exercises? That is, do you gradually expand the practice range, or do the Marchesi exercises accomplish this later?

Each student is individual. Regarding keeping the student in a limited range—the range progresses very gradually, half step by half step in a voice until the voice begins to develop. Then the ranges (low and high) develop a whole step and sometimes a step and one-half in a week's time until the ultimate range of that voice is reached. Some students practice between lessons regularly and with complete concentration. They always progress faster. I do not use Marchesi until they are quite well along.

What about the effect of the emotions on the voice? I know a thirty year old man whose voice was exceedingly "tight"—as was his whole body—until he fell in love. With that some of his vocal problems began immediately to vanish—or rather *the* problem—extreme tension.

Emotions have a tremendous effect on the voice. Sadness, depression, worry—all cause cords to become less flexible (to stiffen). Happiness always manifests itself in the voice. Dr. Miller said:

> The virile, soul-searching appeal of a beautiful, vibrant voice is a manifestation of a sexual embellishment–intended by nature to attract–just as does the song of a bird; the strident chirp of an insect; the roar of the lion. In other words, song is fundamentally a love call, and it can be set down as almost axiomatic that no man or woman ever achieved high distinction in his art who was not, first of all, well sexed, vibrant with life or replete with

the magnetism which is as much an expression of sex virility as is the spreading tail of the peacock.[1]

Where can I buy diagrams of the vocal cords and diaphragm?

Get them from a medical book, or see Chapter 3.

Why do you have the student "hook" every once in a while during the lesson?

To be sure he is releasing the lower abdomen and to get the breath action correct. The "clutch" one feels at the top of the pubic bone on the "k" is the beginning of *all* tone control. (See Chapter 6.)

What do you do about bobbing heads?

Students who bob their heads usually do this to emphasize an emotion or the pulse of the rhythm. They simply have to be trained not to do this. The head should never bob, nor should it be used to accent words. It should never feel rigid, however.

You said to cough instead of clearing your throat, but at one session you said that the vocal cords pull in the same manner when you laugh, cough, yell, or clear the throat.

When I spoke of clearing the throat and then spoke of "coughing" lightly to clear it, this is a different kind of cough. It is simply a puff of air over the cords, much like a "hook." (Chapter 1.)

Regarding the belting exercise: (1) Is the nose held throughout the exercise, or just on the first part? (2) Is this exercise just to be done on those occasions when a belting tone is required, or should it be done every day with the other exercises? (3) Can one do the belting exercise and still retain—at will—the regular "concert" tone?

(1) The nose is held throughout the exercise. (2) This exercise is good for more than just belting: it helps bring the tone into focus. I do not use it every day, however, with the other exercises. (3) One can do the belting exercise and also retain the concert tone *if* he continues all the other exercises and concert literature. (See Chapter 7.)

Do your advanced students do the same exercises?

Yes. They always start with the basics for beginning warm-ups.

---

[1]Frank E. Miller, *Vocal Art Science* (New York, G. Schirmer, Inc., 1922).

How can a choral conductor achieve a healthy vocal sound from a young alto section? Untrained altos usually cannot project in the alto range without breathiness.

Young altos often have no focus to their tone. Use the "preh" exercises (Figure 33) and "ning-ee, ning-ah" (Figure 28) to get the tone farther forward and do not try for "projection." It comes! When you *try* for it, you usually cause pushing. (See Chapter 6.)

What is the "chest voice"? Where is it placed?

When the tone comes directly through the oral cavity with no "dome" or "arch" in it, it is a raw chest tone. However, the low range always has more "chest" in it than higher notes, but it should *always* have head voice in it (dome sensation).

In a Junior High chorus of 45 students, one soprano projects magnificently but she continually sings flat. What is the best way to correct this?

When one sings flat, as your soprano who "projects beautifully," she may be pushing or forcing the voice. The tone must be in balance (front *and* back pull-ups). Use "preh" (Figure 33) and wide snuffs (Figure 47).

How can I encourage my Junior High chorus to project more—i.e., sing out more when in public?

If one tries to get a group or an individual to "sing out" more, he usually gets less tone because the student forces and pushes, causing constriction in the throat. Concentrate on support and diction and they *will* project more. (Chapter 5.)

I have a ninth grade girl student who has a very breathy tone quality that's hardly improved since seventh grade, even with diaphragm exercises. Any suggestions on how to deal with "super-breathy" voices?

I am wondering what "diaphragm exercises" you are using. Breath support is extremely important for eliminating breathiness, and the exercises for breath control given in this book are imperative. Also, at this age level one finds more breathiness, but this gradually disappears as the breath and tone become coordinated and when the resonance comes into the voice. One must not *force* this to happen. (See Chapter 6.)

Why does it hurt voices to take out the vibrato for a white tone?

One restricts the muscles of the soft palate and laryngeal area and this is always harmful.

Can a voice be resonant and yet have no vibrato?

I do not believe so.

During the "ng" and wide snuff exercises, do you breathe through both your nose and mouth?

No. In the first half of the wide snuff, one should breathe only through the nose; the tongue is up in the back of the mouth to block the air from going through the mouth. (See Chapter 7.)

(1) Is there any scientific evidence that the tonsils have anything to do with voice production? (2) Should they be removed?

(1) When tonsils are abnormally large, they block off some of the pharyngeal space and the tone is not as full as it could otherwise be.

(2) Leave tonsils in unless they are so badly diseased that they are causing illness or so large that they are pulling down on the soft palate and closing space in the back of the oral cavity. (See Chapter 13.)

What is a good exercise to strengthen the abdominal muscles to prevent shaking that occurs during singing?

The hook, s-s-s, circle arm (Figures 37-40) and sit-ups (See Chapters 6 and 7). Perhaps the reason the abdominal muscles are shaking is that you are forcing the tone or the singing material is too difficult for you.

How many times should one do the exercises? Does the number increase as one progresses?

Each exercise is done three, four, or five half steps, then change to another exercise. Remember that you are warming up the tiny muscles controlling the vocal cords as well as the soft palate, etc. One does not increase the times one does the exercises as he progresses.

What should the tongue be doing during singing?

It should always be wide, loose and forward against the lower front teeth. On "a," "ay," "ee," "eh," and "ih," it arches, but you do not have to arch it. It is always inside the mouth, however.

Does physical size have a direct relationship to voice size? Can a petite person sing Wagner?

I have never heard a petite person sing Wagner, but I have heard smaller-bodied people who have very "telling" voices—a voice does not need to be big to be beautiful. For a big voice, the body (torso) has become wider from deep breathing and the shape of the face also has a great deal to do with the larger tone. Usually, singers with large voices have almost barrel-like chests.

How long before a performance should one eat? How much should one eat? Does warm or hot liquid actually help the voice or just relax muscles?

Eat two or three hours before singing. Each individual is different as to the amount. I once saw Flagstad eating between acts of an opera. Mint tea with honey is good as it warms the muscles of the whole throat. Any warm liquid does help the voice by relaxing muscles of the throat and making the soft palate more supple.

How long before a performance should one be silent?

Most of the day. (See Chapter 11.)

Regarding not listening to oneself, what if one practices incorrectly?

One would have to go by the sensation created. One should have *no* physical feeling in the throat.

How do these exercises affect a woman during pregnancy and after delivery?

They are good because they help the abdominal muscles to become stronger. After delivery, do not begin singing the heavy material until the body has its strength back.

Is it helpful to lift weight for support while singing?

No!

How do you know when you are keeping your head level?

You may have to watch in a mirror at first because you are unaccustomed to the feeling of the correct position. (See Chapter 4.)

Can a "small" or "nasal" voice be developed into a larger voice, or are certain voices always restricted?

Yes, to the first part of the question: all voices can grow. However, there is a certain physical limitation in some cases. One never knows until correct study is followed.

Why does the "ng" increase range?

It is working on the inside pull-ups that, when developed, help the range.

Are all of the basic exercises safe to use with young Junior High School voices?

All of the first basic exercises (See Chapter 6) are perfectly safe with the exception of ''ng.''

If one is having problems with inflammation of the vocal cords, can a throat specialist take care of the problem?

He can certainly help, but find out *why* they are inflamed and eliminate the cause and don't speak or sing if it is a constant condition. Go to a laryngologist. (See Chapter 3.)

Should the tongue be behind my bottom teeth and touching the roof of the mouth during the ''ng''?

The tip should be behind the teeth, but the back does not have to touch the roof of the mouth. (See Figure 32.)

Do you consider it important to show the student both the right and wrong way to produce a sound?

I think it is helpful. That is one reason why I made the vocal video tapes, ''Basic Components of Singing.''

I can hear that the sound is produced better when using the upper lip. But why does this technique look so unnatural?

The upper lip exercises will gradually strengthen those ''front pull-ups'' until one does not see unnaturalness on the outside. The strength has been developed *inside* the lip muscle. (See Chapter 7.)

What is the best way to sing runs and gain flexibility?

When one gets the back spaces opened, the front pull-ups working together, and correct breath support developed, the flexibility is there. (See Chapter 11.)

How can one be sure of doing the exercises correctly?

By watching in a mirror and feeling that the tone is free. The tone has a *spin* to it.

What do you mean by letting the jaw swing lightly?

Do not "press it down" or have any muscular feeling in it. (See Chapter 8.)

What is the purpose of the uvula? How will its removal (during a tonsillectomy) affect the singing voice?

The uvula allows more muscular tissue to come into use as the soft palate goes up. Scar tissue from a tonsillectomy on the soft palate sometimes restricts the agility of the soft palate. (See Chapter 8.)

Should one think about lowering the larynx while singing? Is this vocally healthy?

No. The larynx adjusts itself when breath support is correct and your jaw and tongue action are correct. (See Chapter 8.)

Some teachers have a student "waggle" the jaw in order to check for tension. Would you recommend this technique?

No! The jaw should always move straight up and down and feel loose. (See Chapter 8.)

What is the purpose of starting the "hee-ah" exercise with an "h"?

"H" is an aspirant and "hooks" into the lower abdominal area which is so important for the lower support of the breath. (See Chapter 6—Figure 23.)

Should the ribs expand with the final quick expulsion of breath on the circle arm breath exercise?

Yes. (See Chapter 7.)

Where is the hard palate?

Run your tongue from behind the front upper teeth backward. The front part is the hard palate, which feels hard. The soft palate is further back. (See Chapter 3.)

To eliminate breathiness, is it correct to carry full chest voice up to the passaggio area of the voice?

Never carry full chest voice up! Work from the head voice down. I do not use the term "passaggio" because I like to feel there are no *breaks* in the vocal line. I constantly speak of ranges—where the tone "sits"—and the tone goes into the vocal line with no problem. The breathiness is eliminated when breath support is right and resonance comes into the voice through these exercises. If the breathiness is caused from oversinging or incorrect singing, this will be eliminated by correcting the cause.

Is it good to take throat lozenges that contain anesthetic if the throat hurts and you must sing?

Never take lozenges which contain anesthetic and then try to sing. It is better not to sing if the throat is hurting. (See Chapter 1.)

If a choir rehearses in a confined area, what can be done to warm them up both physically and mentally?

Rag doll, shoulder stretch, "hook" and circle arm breath. (See Chapter 12.) These exercises will get the blood circulating and mental attitude will automatically change for the better.

How long should the daily warm-up period be for a choir (including body alignment, breathing, and vocalization)? Which vocalises should be used?

This depends on the age level of the choir. For adults, I would say ten to twelve minutes; for younger choirs, eight to ten minutes. Use all the basic exercises, plus snuff-zoh and zah. (See Chapters 6, 7 and 12.)

What type of chairs are best for singing?

Flat bottomed chairs. If they are not available, have students sit on the edges of their chairs with correct body alignment. (See Figure 101.)

Is it best to explain the purpose of each exercise before giving it to a choir?

Not necessarily, but one can if time permits. (See Chapter 12.)

How do you get a blended vocal tone from each section?

The tone will blend when you get that breath support and inside smile with the whole group. (See Chapter 12.)

How can you help students in a choir to sing high notes more easily?

Breath support first; body into the tone (legs supporting); jaw swinging on each high pitch from the width created by the inside smile; and putting consonants on the bottom of intervals.

What can a choir director do to get very small, breathy voices to come alive and stay free? Are there any guidelines you can suggest for the first two or three weeks of working with such a choir?

I find the basic exercises (Chapter 6)—with emphasis on body alignment (Chapter 4)—imperative.

Would you explain how the snuff-up exercise is used for correct vowel sounds?

It creates the open throat and nasal cavity for vowels and consonants. The snuff is through the nose, the lower abdomen springing out as one snuffs. (See Figure 51.)

Why are some people able to roll ''r's'' and others not? What can be done to improve this ability?

Some people simply cannot roll ''r's.'' One can help this problem by involving the upper lip and saying ''trah'' or ''d-t'' rapidly.

What can I do to help a ninth grade female singer with a range of a major sixth, F below middle C up to D? She has no high notes and sings in a chest voice.

Get the ''hook'' exercise started for the breath and begin with the middle or lower part of her range with each of the first six exercises. Let her keep the tone heady, not forced. (See Chapter 6.)

Is it safe to put a young boy soprano into a choir?

If the director understands the young boy's voice and gives material within the comfortable range for this type of voice.

Should a young child be given voice lessons?

A girl usually could begin lessons at twelve or thirteen. Boys can be trained if they are boy sopranos or altos, but then they should be left alone until their voices have changed.

How can a choir director classify voices into SATB and, more importantly, first and second soprano, first and second alto, etc.?

Basically, by the color of the tone—the timbre. It is wrong to have sopranos singing alto just because no one else can read alto or hear the part. High baritones singing tenor can injure their voices. Don't sacrifice voices in order to have your choral group balanced. Re-audition members mid-semester through the period of voice change (Junior and Senior High School level).

You give the impression that if all the pull-ups are not working, the breath capacity and support are diminished.

Right. The vocal line is higher and takes less breath when the pull-ups are involved.

What is the connection between these pull-ups and abdominal support? Is it strictly mental?

No, it is physical. One should always feel the muscles of the lower abdominal area being involved.

Why does exhaling while singing cause such rapid collapse of the abdomen?

The abdomen should never collapse. The stronger the intercostal and lower abdominal muscles become, the less they give in or allow the rapid collapse of the abdomen.

When doing the windmill exercise, do you inhale on one complete circle of the arm and exhale on the next circle? Do you inhale through the nose or the mouth on this exercise?

Inhale as the arm goes in front and up, and exhale as the arm comes down. Inhale through the nose, exhale through the mouth.

Does a thyroid deficiency or imbalance affect the voice? Are there any suggestions or exercises that can be helpful?

Yes, the thyroid balance has a tremendous effect on the voice. Vocal exercises will not help if your thyroid is out of balance.

How can a teacher eliminate an unpleasant "edge" or brittle, sharp sound in a pupil's voice?

Getting the nasal cavity, oral cavity, and pharyngeal areas open.

What is the criterion for basing the starting note of each exercise?

I suppose you mean range-wise. I start in the *low-middle* range with each voice (See Chapter 5.)

What is the rationale for the choice of vowels on the hee-ah-ee-ah exercise?

The "ee" is our most focused vowel. It gets the tone to start front. The "ah" is the most open vowel we have. The exercise allows the vocal mechanism to run the full gamut of activity on these lower pitches.

Is it correct that the muscles of the lips, throat, and face should never be tense? Is this especially true of the "hook" exercise?

Yes, it is always true. Tenseness around the lips on the "hook" exercise causes tenseness in the throat area.

Is it possible to do the "hook" exercise too much?

At one time, yes. Do it a number of times during the day. Teachers illustrating the exercise should be careful not to harm their own bodies overdoing it.

Is the "k" of the "hook" exercise used to expel the rest of the air and trigger the spring-out process?

Yes, one feels a "clutching" at the top of the pubic bone when the "k" is whispered. (See Chapter 6.)

When should movement occur in the chest area during the "hook" exercise?—and what kind of movement?

Sometimes the chest will not move at all or it will go down. It will gradually begin to move and finally come up on the "hook." The exercise will strengthen the abdomen and chest.

The tongue is arched on the inhalation of the wide snuff exercise—is it arched on the exhalation also?

No! It is wide and level on the exhalation. During inhalation, the tongue is simply touching the roof of the mouth in front of the molar teeth. During exhalation, the air comes through the mouth, so the tongue must be wide and lying in the floor of the mouth.

You have mentioned that your speaking voice should be used in the same way as the singing voice. Sometimes when I speak all day, I feel a scratchiness in my throat near the end of the day. I'm wondering if this could be from speaking from my throat? About conversational speaking—when you are talking quietly to another person, do you need to be conscious of the inside smile, etc.?

When your throat feels a scratchiness at the end of the day, you can be certain you have not been speaking correctly. Your breath support should always be there, and the spaces of the oral cavity, nasal cavity, and pharynx should be open. Be sure you are not tightening the jaw at the hinge. When the body becomes fatigued, it is more important to think of breath support, because when breath support is *not* there, the throat muscles begin to work and this brings on the ''scratchiness.''

When you are speaking quietly with another person, you must think of all the components mentioned for singing. Many times it is the ''quiet talking'' done without these components which will harm the voice the most.

What causes the laryngeal area to shake when singing?

The breath support is not complete and the front and back pull-ups are not as strong as they can be and possibly there is pressure on the back of the tongue.

What causes the veins on the side of the neck to stand out when singing?

Forcing will cause this, but other causes can be lack of breath support or a malformation of a vein.

Is whispering ever harmful—particularly when there is a laryngeal condition?

Yes! Whispering is harder on the throat than speaking. One must learn to whisper correctly if necessary for a theatrical production. The correct way to whisper is to leave the throat entirely open and let the consonants be distinctly articulated with the tongue and teeth, and with great support from the ''hook'' area of the abdomen.

"WITHOUT GREAT TEACHERS, GREAT SINGERS CANNOT BE"[2]

---

[2]Ibid.

CONCLUSION

A teacher can devastate a student or build confidence. It is unwise to tell students what we feel it is possible for them to do until we, as teachers, evaluate the level of musicianship, dedication, and self-discipline that a student possesses. It is also wise to know the student's age, ambitions, musical background and whether an operatic career is the ultimate goal. One's background in languages is also very important. How wonderful it is when we find a great instrument in the student who has all the other ingredients: musicianship, dedication, and self-discipline.

We teachers certainly should analyze a student's voice as we hear it the first time and be aware of the student's potential or seeming lack of it. I say "seeming" because we are often fooled by a tiny, insignificant voice which then goes far beyond our expectations. These students are invariably those who are completely dedicated to the art of singing. On the other side of the coin is the student who has a fantastic instrument but lacks discipline in many areas of his life, thereby never attaining success to the same degree as the seemingly lesser gifted person.

Our students should never be belittled for doing something incorrectly. If a student is singing an exercise or a text incorrectly, a teacher should stop and explain why the tone is not "sitting" right. Invariably, when the student understands the reason and uses that approach, he will immediately feel the different sensation and will say, "That feels so easy. In fact, I don't feel like I'm doing anything at all."

It is important to stress, however, that a voice is not built overnight. Patience is imperative and it has its reward. Let me emphasize again that the student must go only one step at a time in overcoming vocal obstacles. A student should not be burdened with thinking about too many things at once. By following the sequence of exercises as given in this text, satisfactory results will come much faster.

The exercises given in this book, though truly simple, will really build voices when done correctly. I feel totally confident in making this statement. Not only have I had a fine singing career of my own, but among my students I have had first place winners in international competitions, and my students are continuing to win awards. Just this year a student who has been with me for two years was given the Martha Baird Rockefeller award of $3,000. She told me that when she started doing these exercises she could not imagine how they could ever build a voice. But after about six months of study she found that her voice "warmed up" faster and more easily than with any other technnique she had ever used. She also found that she could go into the text faster and with more ease.

One should try to be honest with his students when they ask direct questions about what they can expect of their voices, remembering, of course, that none of us knows that answer for sure. Consider one of the greatest contraltos who ever lived, Ernestine Schumann-Heink. She was told to forget a career and to stay at home and rear her children. What a loss it would have been to the world if she had listened to those who gave her such advice.

There are certain essentials which are necessary for building a technique. Once again I wish to stress the importance of learning to analyze the exercises and knowing the correct way they are to be done, rather than just doing them in a haphazard way and expecting results. There is no "guess work" in this technique when the exercises are done properly. Complete concentration is absolutely necessary during the fifteen to thirty minutes of vocalizing in a warm-up, and also while singing the text. It is then possible for the technique to become automatic. The breath is the foundation of the technique and is all-important.

The middle range must be developed first, then followed by the upper and lower ranges. One must approach the text simply at first, with no thought of sentiment or expression. Without technique there is no interpretation. Too often we find our students stressing expression or interpretation before they understand the techniques which best help to bring about that interpretation. Many times students rush to sing a text before they can even speak it in rhythm. Ths sort of approach only retards their progress. "Every art consists of a technical-mechanical part and an aesthetical part. A singer who cannot overcome the difficulties of the first part can never attain perfection on the second, not even a genius."[1]

How thankful I am for the patience of Maude Douglas Tweedy! I cannot refrain from saying this once more at the close of this book. She knew what she was doing. Not once did she praise me or discourage me during the first three years that I worked with her. However, I knew immediately that my throat was relieved of the ache which I carried with me for the three years prior to finding her. I thank the Lord that I found her when I did and that she accepted me as a

---

[1]*Marchesi Vocal Method, Opus 31—Part 1, Elementary and Progressive Exercises; Part 2, Development of the Exercises in the form of Vocalises*, (New York, G. Schirmer, Inc.), used by permission of G. Schirmer, Inc.

student even though my voice was in a real "mess"—which is the best word I can use to describe it. She not only saved my voice, which has provided me with a wonderful singing and teaching career, but she also saved my life!

I hope to have conveyed two important messages in this book: When one uses the natural coordination of the whole body, singing is done easily with no forcing of tone; and singing is one of the most healthful occupations any human being can ever be engaged in.

May this book have important results for those who use it, as the techniques herein have been important to me during forty years of application.

APPENDIX 1

MARCHESI IN DETAIL: THE USE OF
SUPPLEMENTARY EXERCISES

The learning and assimilation of basic technique, and the exercises used to learn that technique, should be accompanied by the study of some of the classical vocalises and exercises that have been used through many decades by many fine singers and instructors.

Each student is so individual that setting a time limit on progress is impossible. Some students start off with better muscular coordination and sharper concentration than do others. Therefore, after approximately six months of study, classical vocalises (such as the Mathilde Marchesi volumes) should be made part of the student's course of study. Because of the details in the studies, I feel that Marchesi is more comprehensive than other classical vocalises. This is why I have felt no need of using any others.

The study of the early Italian classical literature will give the singer a chance to sing in a relatively safe vocal range as he learns to implement the technique he is building. The study of Marchesi's classical vocalises and exercises should be started only after the basic exercises described in this book have built the vocal line and breath support. This will help the singer acquire a natural agility and a basic strength that are necessary to coloring and ornamenting. At this point, the Marchesi volumes will give many vocal exercises which, if practiced diligently, will teach every singer how to develop flexibility and how to control and correctly use that flexibility. In order to integrate the Marchesi exercises with the technique described in this book, it is best to follow the descriptions given below.

As I have mentioned many times, the soft palate is one of the most important anatomical structures in the vocal mechanism. It is directly involved in the singing of scales and arpeggios and is indispensible when ornamenting. The study of the Marchesi volumes can be instituted only after the soft palate has been fairly well strengthened and the breath support strengthened and properly controlled. The appropriate Marchesi volumes will help to coordinate the breath with tone production as well as increase the ability for singing extended phrases and adding ornamentation.

All of the ornaments (mordents, trills, turns, arpeggios, portamentos, etc.) add to the coloring and phrasing of a song and make singing as beautiful and supple as it should be. Without the strength of the soft palate and complete breath control, ornamenting and maintenance of a steady vocal line are virtually impossible to attain.

Instruction employing the Marchesi volumes should begin with *Elementary Progressive Exercises for the Voice, Opus 1,* [1] for all voices. These exercises plus many other excellent exercises also can be found in *Bel Canto: A Theoretical and Practical Vocal Method,* by Marchesi. [2] The exercises should be transposed down for the mezzo-soprano and baritone, about one and one-half tones, and two and one-half tones for the bass and alto. The exercises that I use in *Opus 1* are useful for increasing agility and development of coloratura technique.

Usually, study in *Opus 1* should begin with Exercise 8, useful for increasing agility; it should be transposed up a half step each time it is sung through. Care should be taken not to extend the range too high. One should start with "nee" and go to "ah" on the sixth, allowing the jaw to swing slightly from the hinge on the "ah" emphasizing the inside smile.

He should continue with exercises 9, 10, 11, and 12, changing from "nee" to "ah" on the top pitch of each exercise. On exercises 13, 14, 15, and 16, the jaw should not be allowed to start opening too soon (before reaching the next to top pitch of the scale) so the jaw can swing slightly as it goes to the top pitch. A strong upper lip is vitally important at the bottom of each scale, and the back spaces are always open.

Exercise 17 trains one to release a pitch with ease. If the singer will think of the breath going past the last pitch of an ascending passage as it is released, the throat will never close, causing the tone to be difficult to release. In the upper range the jaw should be allowed to swing open very slightly as the pitch is released.

Exercise 18 should be started on "nee"; as one descends into the low range, he should think the tone into the teeth, with the sternum coming up very strongly, as a result of the lower abdominal muscles coming in, thus giving support to the tone. He should change to "ah" on the last pitch and swing the jaw *slightly* as the pitch is released. When he has moved into the upper-middle

---

[1] Mathilde Marchesi, *Elementary Progressive Exercises for the Voice,* Opus 1, Vol. 384, (New York, G. Schirmer, Inc., 1881)

[2] Mathilde Marchesi, *Bel Canto: A Theoretical and Practical Vocal Method* (New York, Dover, 1970)

and high range, he should start the top of the scale on "nah" and go into "nee" at the bottom.

The advanced singer can sing exercises 19-24 and 35-40 on the word "boo," taking a breath as needed at first, then later trying to sing the exercise on as few breaths as possible. Eventually the exercise will be easily sung in one breath through to the last measure. Caution: A soft "b" should be used, not an explosive "b." Usually the "oo" is easily sung by a coloratura voice. However, if the student has a difficult time with the "oo," he should leave these alone until he has worked with the "koo, koo, koo" exercises (Figures 43 and 44).

On the first measure of exercise 25, the singer should start with "nee" and portamento up to the octave and change to "ah." He should begin in low range, being certain that the bottom pitch always has strength across (but never a pulling up of) the upper lip. The mask is already wide on the bottom pitch so the upper pitch will pop in easily as the jaw is swung, but not too far. Each bottom note should then be on "nee"—each top note on "ah."

In exercise 26, the first pitch should be on "nah" and the octave drop is on "ee." (After the first "n" it should not be repeated.)

One should then skip to exercise 29, sung on "nah." The purpose of this exercise is to learn to release the upper pitch—the same as exercise 17 only more difficult. When the singer reaches the last two octaves, he should be sure that he does not drop his jaw before he gets into the upper-middle range so that there is space left to release the jaw on the top pitch. The mask must be involved at the bottom of every ascending scale so that the upper pitch will always be easy.

In exercise 30, sing "nah" down to "ee." The feeling of the snuff exercise (Figure 51) is involved on the attack of the top pitch of the descending scale. Also, in the upper range of the voice, the singer should always be sure he allows a muscle flow from his legs through his body.

Exercises 31 and 32 involve the same principles. Omit exercises 33 and 34.

Exercises 35-40 involve more advanced coloratura singing, sung using the same principles as outlined above.

Exercise 41 is sung on "nah." It is good for getting the jaw to swing loosely from the back (with an inside smile). The jaw drops slightly on the first pitch and swings slightly more open on the second pitch, back to the first position on the third and swinging on four, etc., up the scale. This is training the hinge of the jaw to swing loosely on any interval. As the strength of the inside smile is developed, less movement of the jaw will be necessary on smaller intervals—thirds, fourths, fifths, sixths. Skips of sevenths on up must always have more swing in the jaw.

Exercise 42 should be sung on "nah." The jaw never has any feeling of weight or pushing down. It always swings from a feeling of width of mask.

When the student has mastered the basic principles I have given in this book and applied them, the rest of the exercises are easily learned.

Exercises 71 and 72 are to strengthen and help the student become aware of how important it is to have strength in the upper lip as he is singing scales requiring agility. They should be sung on "nah." To illustrate the difference, try to sing these exercises with the upper lip pulled down. Tones do not articulate as easily. The jaw moves slightly on the third tone. If the jaw is stiff, tones will not move as easily.

Before starting exercise 133, always begin with "koo" (Figures 43 and 44). The "koo" will have activated the soft palate in such a way that when exercise 133 is sung on "boo" one will feel the same sensations felt on "koo." The soft palate should be allowed to be very flexible, and the lips should never be tightened on the "oo"—they should only be slightly rounded.

The last exercise in the book should then be sung, still on "boo."

Opus 15, entitled *Elementary and Progressive Exercises,*[3] should be given to the bass, baritone and mezzo-soprano, and study should begin on page 8. The first seven pages of Opus 15 are not used here because the basic exercises of the technique described in this book supersede those studies. However, exercises 2 and 3 can be used as simple Italian songs.

It is important to make easy the articulation of the rapid passages. For example, in exercise 4, to sing the "p" of "posso," one must feel a puff of air up under the upper lip (the lip in normal position, and never pressed down). In the second phrase, "il finger," the "g" is soft as in "general" and feels as though it is being pronounced in front of the first molar tooth, the "r" being flipped, with the tip of the tongue being wide and soft. (The upper lip is involved in making the flipped "r" easier.) At the end of the second phrase, in the word "gabbar," the double "b" is voiced by allowing the lips to be brought together loosely enough so that they can vibrate as the "b" is being sung.

Opus 2, *Twenty-Four Vocalises for Soprano or Mezzo-Soprano,*[4] should be given preferably to the mezzo-soprano and possibly to the soprano. The study of Opus 2 is begun on exercise 5.

One will wish to alternate the vowels from phrase to phrase between "nee," "nah," "noo," and "boo." A whole exercise should never be sung

[3]Mathilde Marchesi, *Elementary and Progressive Exercises,* Opus 15, Vol. 593 (Medium Voice), (New York, G. Schirmer, Inc., 1926)

Mathilde Marchesi, *Elementary and Progressive Exercises,* Opus 15, Vol. 594 (Alto Voice), (New York, G. Schirmer, Inc., 1926)

[4]Mathilde Marchesi, *Twenty-Four Vocalises for Soprano or Mezzo-Soprano,* Opus 2, Vol. 391 (New York, G. Schirmer, Inc., 1926)

on one vowel. (One should never sing a song through on one vowel as he is learning it, either.)

One should also be sure to apply the scientific principles of skips of intervals: (1) the jaw always swings slightly (or if it is a wider interval, more); and (2) in an ascending interval, the bottom of the interval must be as high in position in the inside of the oral cavity as the upper part of the interval will be when it is attained.

APPENDIX 2

DEFINITIONS

In certain cases, I have used some terms that are not in general usage. They are listed here, with explanations.

Back Spaces: The space around the soft palate and the back of the mouth. This is the feeling we have when the "inside pull-ups" are working.

Cushions: Muscles over the top of the cheek bones and under the eyes. When one is laughing or smiling, these "cushions" are visible on the face.

Front Pull-ups: The muscles on the outside of the face; over the bridge of the nose; the muscles above the upper lip close to the nose; the muscles inside the upper lip, and the muscles one feels when gently snuffing his nose.

Heady Tones: Those tones which have a light quality of sound. They feel as though they go back, up and over the soft palate; the bones of the face or chest are not involved.

Inside Arch: That part of the "inside smile" which gives the feeling of a dome or umbrella in the soft palate and hard palate areas.

Inside Pull-ups: Muscles of the soft palate and hard palate. One feels these muscles when yawning—the top (upward) half of the yawn, never a feeling of yawning pushing down into the throat. It is possible, for certain effects, to use these muscles independently of the "front pull-ups."

Mask: The sets of muscles of the face—under the eyes into the temples, around the flanges of the nose, in the lips, and from the temples down to the chin.

Appendix 3

EXERCISE CHART

(Detailed in Chapters 6 and 7)

BREATHING AND BODY COORDINATION

Hook
Hee-ah (Figure 23)
Hook (Variation)
Hawk (Figures 36a and 36b)
Circle Arm Breath (Figures 37, 38, 39, 40)
S-s-s Breath
Back Breath
Ballet Stretch
Rag Doll
Snuff-zoh-zah (Figures 51-55)

STRENGTHENING THE SOFT PALATE

Kee-kay and kee-kah (Figure 24)
Kah-kay-kee-koh-koo (Figure 41)
Kee-kah-kee (Figure 42)
Koo (Figures 43-44)
Wide Snuff (Figure 47)
Waw-ee (Figure 49)
Heady Nee and nee-ah (Figure 62)

COORDINATION OF TONGUE AND JAW

Flah-flah-nee (Figure 25)
Kee-kah-kee (Figure 42)
Flah-flah-ning-ah (Figure 46)
Thee-thah (Figure 63)
Thah-thee (Figure 64)

FOCUS

Ning-ee and ning-ah (Figure 28)
Ng (Figures 29-31)
Preh (Figure 33)
Kah-kay-kee-koh-koo (Figure 41)
Flah-flah-ning-ah (Figure 46)
Wide snuff (Figure 47)
Ng-ee-ay-ah (Figure 50)
Snuff-zoh-zah (Figures 51-55)
Nee-oh (Figure 58)
Ning-ee and ning-ah (Figure 60)
Ming-mee (Figure 67)
Mee-oh (Figure 69)

BRIDGE OVER RANGES

Ng (Figures 29-31)

EXTENSION OF RANGE

Ng (Figures 29-31)
Wide Snuff (Figure 47)
Hee-ah, hah-ah (Figure 48)
Waw-ee (Figure 49)
Ng ng (Figure 57)
Five-part exercise (Figures 62-66)
Nee-ah-ee-ah-ee-ah-ee (Figure 66a)
Nee-ah (Figures 70-72)

REMOVE SHRILLNESS

Nee-oh-(ay)-(ah)-(eye) (Figure 59)

DEVELOPING STACCATO

Sh-sh-sh (Figure 56)
Ng-ng-ng (Figure 57)

RELATING VOCALISES TO SUNG TEXTS

Lah-bay-dah-may-nee-poh-too (Figure 68)

TONGUE

Thee-thah (Figure 63)
Thah-thee (Figure 64)

Index

A

Abdominal muscles, 43, 54, 58, 66, 67, 71-75, 76, 81, 85-91, 100-103, 121, 135, 137-138, 171-173, 175, 178, 185, 186, 192, 201, 202, 204, 207
Abdominal surgery, 194-195
Abuse, vocal, 27-30, 136
Accompanists, 40, 157-158
Alcohol, 29
Anaptyxis, 198
Anesthesia, 194-195
Announcing of songs, 158
Artistry, vocal, 166
"Ave Maria" from *Otello*, 161-162

B

Back muscles, 66, 73, 90, 99
Back spaces, 221
Balanced tone, 197, 198
Belittling singers, 169, 211
"Belting" tone, 111-112, 165, 199
    See also "Musical theater"

Blend, choral, 205
Body alignment, 41, 53, 57-63, 71, 76, 86, 171-173, 175, 179-180, 184, 186, 191, 194, 205, 206
Body warm-ups, 169-170
Bowing, 157
"Breaks", vocal, 67, 69, 136, 204-205
Breath, suspended, 101
Breathing, 10-11, 52-55, 65-70, 71-75, 121-123, 133, 136-137, 184, 200, 207, 209, 212
"Broadway" tone, see "Belting" tone

C

Caps, tooth, 48
Cavity, nasal, 44
Cavity, oral, 44
Chairs, choral, 175, 205
Chest area, 52-53, 59 (illus), 60, 71, 73, 74, 90, 170, 173, 186, 191-192, 208
Chest voice, 200, 204, 206
Choral exercises, 170-175
Choral singing, 169-181, 205

Classification of voices for choirs, 206

Clearing of throat, 185, 199

Coaches, vocal and dramatic, 40-41, 154-155

Coloratura singing, 75, 93-95, 162, 203, 215-219

Colors, vocal, 117, 155-156, 159-165, 206, 216

Consonants, 10, 47, 73, 146-150, 162, 179, 194, 198, 205, 218

Contests and festivals, 177

Copying other singer's voices, 34, 175, 179

Cords, vocal, 50-52 (illus), 68

Coughing, 199

Cricoid Cartilage, 51 (illus), 52

Cushions, 221

D

Dead pan expression, 35, 38, 39 (illus)

Dentures, 47-48

Diaphragm, 43, 53-55 (illus), 58, 66, 67, 72-73

Diphthongs, 144

Drinking before performances, 202

Dynamic levels, 100-101, 112

E

Eating before performances, 202

Egotism, 159

Elision of words, 146, 197

Emotions, effect on voice, 115-116, 161, 191, 198-199

Erlkönig, Der, 160-161

Exercise, body, 30, 66, 196

Exercises, advanced, 10, 85-113, 201, 211-212

Exercises after vocal rest, 141, 196

Exercises, basic, 10, 71-83, 85, 198, 199, 201, 203, 205, 206, 211-212, 215

Exercises for breathing and body warm-up:

Back breath, 90-91, 223

Exercises for breathing and body warm-up *(cont'd.)*

Ballet stretch, 91, 99, 171, 192, 223

Circle-arm breath, 86-89 (illus), 122, 187, 192, 193, 201, 204, 205, 223

Hah-hay-hee-hoh-hoo, 137-138

Hook, 71-74, 76, 173, 186-188, 192, 193, 194, 199, 201, 205, 206, 208, 223

Hook (variation), 85-86, 223

Rag doll, 95-96, 109, 122, 170, 171, 176, 186, 190, 192, 205, 223

S-s-s, 89, 201, 223

Sit-up, 133, 201

Shoulder exercises, 170-171, 190, 192, 193, 205

Torso exercise, 171, 205

Windmill, 170, 207

Exercises, Marchesi, (see Marchesi exercises)

Exercises for vocal development:

Ah-ah-ah, 119

Fah-ee-ah-ee, Fee-ah-ee-ah, 134, 141, 186-187, 189, 194, 196

Five part exercise, 104-110, 224

Flah-flah, 138

Fla-flah-nee, 76-78, 174, 196, 224

Flah-flah-ning-ah, 95, 224

Gah, 124, 127, 128

Hawk, 86, 223

Hee-ah, 74-75, 122, 173, 204, 207, 223

Hee-ah, Hah-ah, 97-98, 224

Hum-ee, Hum-ah, 140, 141

Hum-mah, Hum-may, 134-135, 141

Hum-mee, Hum-mah, 122-123, 190

Hum portamento, 122, 123

Kah-kay-kee-koh-koo, 91-92, 122, 223, 224

Kah-kee-koh, 135-136, 141

Kee-kah-kee, 92-93, 122, 223, 224

Kee-kay-kee-kah, 138-139, 141

Kee-kay, kee-kah, 75-76, 122, 173-174, 187, 189, 196

Exercises for vocal development *(cont'd.)*
Koo, 93-95, 217-218, 223
Lah-bay-dah-may-nee-poh-too, 111,
188, 190, 192-193, 194, 225
Mah-mah, 139, 141
Mee-oh, 111-112, 164, 165, 199, 224
Ming-mee, 110-111, 224
Nee, Nee-ah, heady (five part exer-
cise), 105-107, 223
Nee-ah (range extension), 112-113,
224
Nee-ah-ee-ah-ee-ah-ee (five part exer-
cise) 108-110, 195, 224
Nee-oh, 103-104, 224
Nee-oh-(ay)-(ah)-(eye), 104, 224
Ning-ee, Ning-ah, 78-79, 141, 200,
224
Ning-ee, Ning-ah (five part exercise),
105, 224
Ng, 78-79, 141, 190, 195, 201, 202-
203, 224
Ng-ah, 124, 127, 187, 192, 193, 194
Ng-ee-ay-ah, 99, 224
Ng-ng-ng, 102-103, 225
Preh, 75, 81-83, 130, 145, 147, 164,
165, 188, 189, 192, 200, 224
Rolled tongue, 119-121, 124
Sh-sh-sh, 102-103, 192, 225
Snuff-zoh-zah, 100-101, 122, 146,
174, 175, 205, 206, 217, 223,
224
Thee-thah, Thah-thee (five part exer-
cise), 106-107, 124, 224, 225
Waw-ee, 98-99, 122, 223, 224
Waw-ee-ah, 122, 123
Wide snuff, 96-97, 98-99, 109, 122,
178, 186-189, 190, 192, 193,
194, 196, 200, 201, 208, 223,
224
Zay-luh, zah-luh, 100-101, 174-175
Eye glasses, 158

F

Facial Muscles, 44
Fatigue, 209

Feet, position of, 57
"Fluted lip" technique, 35-40, 36 (illus)
Focus, 10-11, 78-81, 92, 95, 99, 100-
101, 103-104, 105, 110-111, 145,
165, 199, 200
Forte tones, (see Projection of tone)
Frauenliebe und Leben, 163-164

G

Glottal attacks, 146, 188
Grimacing, 38, 39 (illus), 173
Gums, diseased, 47

H

Hands, use of in choral directing, 178-
179
Hansel and Gretel, 164
Head, position of, 59 (illus), 62-63 (il-
lus), 176, 199, 202
Head voice, 93-95, 105-107, 160, 162,
196, 200, 204, 206
Heady tones, 221
Health, physical, 10, 27, 30, 141
Hollinshead, Henry, 66
"Hook muscle," 73, 102-103, 147, 209,
(see also Abdominal muscle)
Humor in choral rehearsals and lessons,
169, 173, 178, 194
Hyoid bone, 45 (illus), 47, 49 (illus), 50,
115
Hypopharynx, 49 (illus), 50

I

Insecurity, 159
Inside smile, explanation of, 35, 37, 38
(illus), 40, 128, 139-140, 148, 173,
221
Inside smile, use of, 10-11, 35, 44, 47,
68, 71, 75, 76, 78, 81, 89, 92, 95,
102, 107, 108-109, 111-112, 134-
135, 138, 146, 153, 179, 187, 189,
194, 217
Involuntary nervous system, 52, 54, 68,
128

J

Jaw, 43, 68, 69, 75, 76-78, 81, 92, 95,
    104, 107, 108-109, 115, 119, 121,
    127-128, 138, 147-148, 174, 184,
    192, 194, 204, 209, 216, 217, 218,
    219
Jaw, problems of, 115, 130-136

K

Knee, flexed position, 57-58 (illus), 60,
    171-173
Kobbe, Gustav, 165

L

Languages, foreign, 153-155, 211
Laryngopharynx, (see hypopharynx)
Larynx, 47, 48, 50-52 (illus), 204
Larnyx, manipulation of, 52, 115, 204
Lifting weight while singing, 202
Line, vocal, 67-68, 130, 143, 153, 155-
    156, 205, 207, 215
Lip, upper, 77-78, 82-83, 104, 105 (il-
    lus), 109, 110-111, 128-130 (illus),
    147, 197, 203, 206, 216, 218
Lips, 68, 95, 218
Literature, vocal, 85
Lowen, Harry J., 43
Lungs, 52-55

M

Marchesi exercises, 198, 215-219
Marchesi, Mathilde, 212, 215-219
"Marking," 29
Mask (see also "Inside smile"), 44, 75,
    77-78, 81, 92, 98-99, 102, 104,
    108-109, 110-111, 121, 130, 144,
    147, 173, 191, 194, 217, 221
Menstruation, 30
Microphones, 179-180
Mikado, The, 164
Miller, Frank E., 11, 116, 123, 140-141,
    143, 146-147, 155, 161, 165-166,
    183, 198-199, 209

Mucus, 45-46, 52, 185
Music, selection of, 177, 178
Musical theater, 177-178, (see also
    "Belting tone")

N

Nasal cavity, 44-46, 75, 79, 80, 81-83,
    96-97, 100-101, 111-112, 117,
    144, 164, 165, 188, 206, 209
Nasal tones, 115, 116-118, 164
Nasopharynx, 44, 49-50 (illus), 80, 105,
    117-118, 120, 147
Nodes, vocal, 136-140 (illus), 184
Note-taking at lessons, 33

O

Oral cavity, 47-48, 209, 219
Organists, 180
Ornaments (see Coloratura singing)
Oropharynx, 38, 47, 49 (illus), 50, 201

P

Pain deadeners, 29, 205
Palate, hard, 45, 47, 48, 49, 80, 144,
    204, 221
Palate, soft, 43, 45, 46 (illus), 123, 132,
    138-139, 173, 200, 204, 215, 218,
    221
Pants roles, 162
Patience in teaching, 165-166, 211
Performance, day of, 157, 202
Pharynx, 48-50 (illus), 96, (see also
    Hypopharynx, Oropharynx, and
    Nasopharynx)
Physical size, 201-202
"Pill," The, 30
Pitch, 115, 188, 192, 193
Polyps, 183-184
Posture, (see Body alignment)
Practice rooms, 41
Practicing, 29, 41
Pregnancy, 30, 202
Problems, vocal, 10, 83, 115-141, 183-
    196, 203

Projection of tone, 11, 67, 75, 81, 111-
    112, 117, 119, 130, 174, 188, 200
Pronunciation guide, 19
Psychological problems, effect of on
    voice, 116, 191
"Pull-ups, Front," 203, 207, 209, 221
"Pull-ups, inside," 44, 75, 132, 197,
    202-203, 207, 209, 221

Q

"Quiet speaking," 209

R

Ranges, voice, 58, 68-69, 79-81, 96-99,
    104-110, 112-113, 153, 160-161,
    165, 176-177, 198, 202-203, 204-
    205, 206, 212, 216
Recorders, tape, 42
Registers, (see Ranges)
Release of tone, 216-217
Resistance, concept of, 187
Resonance (see Projection of tone)
Rib cage, 73, 87, 90-91, 96, 196
Rock singing, 165
Rolling "R's," 206, 218

S

Scar tissue, 195-196
Septum, 44, 45, 49 (illus), 103
Shoulders, position of, 59-60 (illus), 66,
    73, 74, 76, 172-173 (illus), 186
Shrillness, 104
Size of voice, 201, 202
Smoking, 29
Songs and Dances of Death, 163
Speaking techniques, 208-209
Staccato singing, 102-103
Stage deportment and performance, 157-
    158
Stage fright, 159
Sternum, 53, 102, 216
Support, body, 10-11, 65-70, 209, 215,
    216

Surgery, 194-196
Swayback problem, 60-61

T

Tailbone, position of, 57, 171-173, (see
    also Body alignment)
Teacher, selection of, 34-35
Teaching, art of, 211-213
Teaching studio, 41
Teaching, importance of, 9, 154-155,
    159-160, 175
Techniques, combining, 35
Tension, 95-97, 198-199, 208
Texts, song, 111, 153-156, 212
Throat, open, 73, 203, 206
Throat, problems of, 183-196, 209
Thyroid cartilage, 51 (illus), 52
Thyroid level, 30, 207
Tongue, 38, 43, 45-46 (illus), 47, 50, 63,
    68, 75, 76-78, 81, 92-93, 95, 104,
    107-109, 118, 119-121, 123-124,
    130, 132, 138, 147-148, 174, 184,
    194, 201
Tongue exercises, 189, 190, 192
Tongue, problems of, 115, 119-121,
    123-128 (illus), 136, 187-188, 192,
    209
Tonsillectomy, 195-196, 201, 204
Tonsils, Palatine, 49 (illus), 50, 117-118
    (illus), 201
Translating of song texts, 33, 154
Transposed music, 178
Trills, (see Coloratura singing)
Tweedy, Maude Douglas, 11, 12, 116,
    212

U

Uvula, 117-118 (illus), 204

V

Vennard, William, 73
Vibrato, 75-76, 99, 100-101, 119, 121-
    123, 179, 200, 201
Visual attention of singer, 158

Vocal cords (folds), 50-52
Vowels, 81-83, 143-146, 179, 206,
    218-219

W

Warm-ups, choral, 169-175, 177, 205

Whispering, 185, 191, 209
Wobble, 115

Y

Yannopoulos, Dino, 155
Young singers, 200, 203, 206